T0196347

PSYCHO-EDUCATIONAL ASSESSMENTS *of*
CHILDREN AND ADOLESCENTS
Practical Suggestions for Teachers, Parents and Students

Joseph Nii Abekar Mensah, PhD

authorHOUSE®

AuthorHouse™
1663 Liberty Drive
Bloomington, IN 47403
www.authorhouse.com
Phone: 1 (800) 839-8640

Published by AuthorHouse 06/22/2017

ISBN: 978-1-5246-9731-0 (sc)
ISBN: 978-1-5246-9729-7 (hc)
ISBN: 978-1-5246-9730-3 (e)

Library of Congress Control Number: 2017909782

Print information available on the last page.

DEDICATION

This book Is Dedicated to the following:

EBENEZER NII SEMPEH MENSAH, Dip. Bus,Admin.

&

My Parents: Nii Larbi Mensah II & Mary
Naa Adoley Ayikailey Addo.
My Children and Grandchildren
All my extended family members

ACKNOWLEDGEMENTS

I acknowledge and thank the Almighty God for His abundant blessings upon me and my family. Words are too weak to express my gratitude to my parents, late Nii Larbi Mensah II (Sempe Mensa We Atofo Mantse), and Mary Naa Adoley-Ayikailey Addo for their love and for being wonderful parents to me and my siblings.

The love and care shown by my paternal and my maternal grandparents are noteworthy, and for their positive influences on my life. I will like to thank also my elder sister, Esther Naa Tettehley Amarteifio; my brother, Joseph Nii Abeka Mensah Jr, as well as all members of my extended family, too numerous to mention individually, for being so kind and loving to me.

Special word of thanks and appreciation to all my children and grandchildren for their love, especially Ebenezer Nii Sempeh, for all the help and care he always gives me.

My beloved children are late Joseph Nii Sempeh Mensah, Gamal Nii Sempeh Mensah, Mrs. Farah Naa Nyarkua Newmarch, Ebenezer Nii Sempeh Mensah and Shelly L.Mensah.

My loving grandchildren are: Barbara Naa Tettehley Mensah, Jeffery Nii Abekar Mensah, Kevin Nii Tetteh Mensah, Tate Nii Adotey Newmarch, Paighton Naa Akaibi Newmarch; Shaelyn Naa Adoley-Ayikailey Newmarch.

Joseph Nii Abekar Mensah, and Joseph Nii Abeka Mensah, Jr. Samantha Ama Mensah and Tyrrell Mensah.

Finally, a word of thanks to the following, whose kindness and friendship will forever linger in my mind: Mr. Kweku and Nancy Edugyan and family, Dr. Ishmael Bruce, late Mr & Mrs Joseph Hagen and family, late Dr. Ishmael Okraku, and Lynette L.Mensah.

ABOUT THE AUTHOR

Dr. Joseph Nii Abekar Mensah was born in Accra, Ghana to Nii Larbi Mensah II, Sempe Mensa We Atofo Mantse, and Mary Naa Adoley-Ayikailey Addo. He received his basic education at Saint Mary's Parish School and Accra Bishop's Boys School. Dr.Mensah then attended Odorgonno Secondary School,Accra. Upon completion of his secondary education, Dr. Mensah was sent by his late father to London, England where he read for the General Certificate of Education Advanced Level. He then attended Barking Regional College of Technology, where he received education in Applied Biology with specialization in Pharmacology.

Following completion of his studies, Dr. Mensah worked as a Research Technologist at London Hospital Medical College, Department of Pharmacology supervised by Dr. C,R.B Joyce; and also as a Research Assistant in endocrinology at the University College Hospital Medical School under Dr. E.J. Ross. Subsequently, Dr. Mensah was employed as a Research Assistant at Union International, London, where he was involved in bioassay of insulin.

Dr,Mensah later immigrated to Canada in October 1968, having been appointed as a Research Technologist. He worked under Dr. Charles R.Dean, conducting bio-assay of neuro-secretory substances at Dalhousie University in Halifax, Nova Scotia, Canada.

While in Halifax, Dr. Mensah earned a Bachelor of Science degree in Psychology and a Bachelor of a Bachelor of Education degree from Saint Mary's University. He is also a graduate of Dalhousie University, Halifax with Bachelor of Arts in Sociology, Graduate Diploma in Public Administration, and a Master of Arts degree in Education. Dr. Mensah also earned a Master's degree in Educational Psychology and Measurements from Mount Saint Vincent University, Halifax

Dr. Mensah is a graduate of Columbia Pacific University, Mill Valley, California, with Master of Science degree in Counselling Psychology and a Doctor of Philosophy degree in Psycho-gerontology.

He has held numerous academic and professional positions. He was a part-time lecturer of education at Dalhousie University, the Nova Scotia Teacher's College, Truro. Dr. Mensah also served as an Adjunct Professor of the University of Santa Barbara and the Columbia Pacific University,

Dr. Mensah has authored a number of books and articles, including, GHANA: HISTORY AND TRADITIONAL CUSTOMS OF A PROUD PEOPLE (Exposition Press, 1981); GADANGMES OF GHANA: HEBRW ISRAELITES ORIGINS AND TADITIONAL CUSTOMS (Aurora Press, 2008); STRESS MANAGRMENT AND YOUR HEALTH (Strategic Book Publishing, 2013); TRADITIONS AND CUSTOMS OF GADANGMES OF GHANA: DESCENDANTS OF AUTHENTIC BIBLICAL HEBREW ISRAELITES (Strategic Book Publishing, 2013)

Dr. Mensah holds professional teaching certifications in the Provinces of Nova Scotia and Alberta, as well as provincial teacher certifications in the Provinces of Ontario and British Columbia

He had been a member of the formerly Psychologists Association of Alberta; the American Psychological Association; the Society for the Psychological study of Social Issues; and the International Council of Psychologists

Dr. Mensah holds Fellow and Diplomate certification with the American Board of Medical Psychotherapists; and a Diplomate certification with the International Academy of Behaviour Medicine, Counselling and Psychotherapy.

PREFACE

This book is written to address concerns of parents, teachers, and students, prior to and after psycho-educational assessments. Parents become very anxious when they receive school's requests for assessment of their child or children. Their anxiety is compounded during and after case conferences, when some parents feel they do not understand what the psychologist is trying to say

Also, I have heard some teachers complain that the test results and accompanying recommendations are too technical; and that they do not comprehend the testing procedures. It is hoped that this book will be easily to read and understood by teachers, parents and students; and addresses most of the concerns of teachers and parents regarding psycho-educational assessments.

Chapter One focuses on the referral question, the assessment procedures, the test results, the interpretations of the test results, and the psychologist recommendations

In Chapter Two, the author addresses Behaviour Disorders in schools and some strategies for combating behaviour disorders in the classroom. Chapter Three focuses on more advanced strategies for dealing with behaviour problems in school.

Chapter Four is concerned about how to deal with youths at-risk in the classroom, and some effective strategies, while Chapter Five focuses on Special Education in schools and issues concerning Special Education.

In Chapter Six, the author dwells on Learning and Developmental Disorders, while in Chapter Seven deals with the issue of minorities in the education system, as well as Development of Community Support System for schools

INTRODUCTION

Many books have been written about education and psychological assessments by great scholars and Clinicians yet, I have not come across books that make the psycho-educational process easily understood by educational personnel in the schools and parents..

This book is intended to help school administrators, teachers, counsellors, support staff, parents and other professionals to read and understand psycho-educational reports, and to work as a team to help alleviate the student's difficulties. Furthermore, this book is aimed as sensitizing the school personnel to the elements of a quality psycho-educational assessment; to make them informed consumers who are able to understand good quality report so as to apply the information contained in the report effectively in the schools.

In general, psycho-educational assessment provides estimates of the student's intellectual or cognitive abilities as well as the client's current performance in the three basic areas of school adjustments namely, Reading, Spelling and Arithmetic. In addition, psycho-educational assessment results in recommendations that may be relevant in educational planning for the student. Assessment data generally include background information obtained from parents and guardian of the student, teachers and school support staff; educational history and records and data from intelligence tests and educational achievement. It may also include data from rating tests of attention disorder evaluation scale, emotional and behaviour problem scales as well as tests of adaptive behaviour.

Psycho-educational assessment is primarily designed to respond to some of the following questions: Does the student have average or better intelligence to benefit from academic work; and what can we learn from the client's test scores to indicate his/her strengths and weaknesses? Is he or she mentally challenged? Does he/she have attention deficit-hyperactive problem? Does the client have emotional/behaviour problems? Is the client learning disabled? Does the assessment data suggest possible neurological and/or neuropsychological difficulties? Is hearing or visual difficulties suggested by the data? What would be the appropriate educational planning for the student in the light of background data and information gathered from the assessment data?

Even though learning, and not behavioural/emotional problems, is the focus of the psycho-educational assessment, emotional/behavioural and medical issues may need to be attended to in psycho-educational evaluation. Referrals to medical or other professionals may be made if necessary.

The format of psycho-educational reports may vary. Most reports include certain basic components. Psycho-educational implies applying psychological theories and techniques in a school setting. Thus, a psycho-educational report is a type of psychological report that focuses on assessment and interpretation of educationally related psychological and educational and psychological tests. These include tests of intelligence, receptive and expressive language,

achievement tests, tests of auditory and visual perception; tests of attention deficit-hyperactive behaviour as well as tests of emotional/behaviour problems, etc. Personality and psychopathology tests may also be administer

CONTENTS

Dedication v
Acknowledgements vii
About The Author ix
Preface xi
Introduction xiii

CHAPTER 1 1
Preparing The Child For Testing 2
Referral Question: 14
Background Information 14
Assessment Procedure 14
General Observation – Test Behaviour 15
Test Results 16
Interpretation of the Test Results. 16
Summary and Recommendations 24
References 27

CHAPTER II 29
Behaviour Disorders In Schools 29
Definition of Behaviour Disorders 31
Identification, Assessment, and Program Planning for the
Behaviourally Disordred Child. 37
References 41

CHAPTER III 44
Corrective Strategies For Behaviour Disorders In School 44

CHAPTER IV 48
How To Deal With Youths At Risk 48
Strategies For Rescuing At-risk Students 51
The Decision Making Process 60
Developmental and Learning Disorders 62

References 74

CHAPTER V 76
Special Education Services 76
Task-Oriented Teaching Behaviours For Special Needs Students. 80
References 84

CHAPTER VI 86
Learning And Developmental Disorders 86
Attention Deficit Disorders. 91
Attention Deficit Disorder With Hyperactivity. 96
Language ProblemsLanguage Problems 100

CHAPTER VII 116
Education Of Ethnic Minorities; Developing Community
Support 116
REFERENCE 122
About the Author 127

CHAPTER 1

PREPARING THE CHILD FOR PSYCHOEDUCATIONAL EVALUATION

Psycho-educational assessments and their results can generate feelings of confusion, despair or relief in parents. These various and rigorous tools are the means by which a determination is made finally after a period of parental frustration about the child's performance in school. Psycho-educational evaluations enable parents to take an important step towards determining the root causes of the child's learning and/or emotional difficulties and finding ways to help the child. Despite the fact that psycho-educational reports can be intimidating to parents and teachers, these reports detail a great deal about the child's strengths and weaknesses, neurological development, and at times, the child's emotional-behaviour problems.

Most parents and some teachers do not really comprehend what the psycho-educational evaluations say about their children other than knowing that the child has been diagnosed for learning problems and/or behavioural-emotional issues. This is deplorable, because a comprehensive psycho-educational testing battery provide so much information about the child which may be used to help the child than a label. It seems to me; therefore, testing is meaningless if parents, teachers and others who work with the child are unable to comprehend the psych-educational test results.

Psycho-educational test results generally detailed important information about the child's natural learning style, detailed by specific strengths and weaknesses. The test administrator, who is generally a registered/certified psychologist may be able to explain to the parent and teachers that the child may have average or better intelligence and has potential to succeed in school. However, the child may have problem with memory, attending and concentration; and that with proper educational programming and support the child will be able to overcome those difficulties and succeed in school. After many months or years of frustration by the parent and the child, it is reassuring for the parent hear the Psychologist reinforce that the child is bright and capable, which is supported by the test results. There may be neuropsychological and/or neurological basis for the challenges confronting the child which, are misunderstood and construed as "laziness" or "unmotivated." It is important to note that no single test can be used to diagnose a child's problem; and no single test score can stand alone to suggest a specific strength or weakness. Rather the psychologist looks for a pattern of strengths and weaknesses that can emerge across several tests.

Preparing The Child For Testing

Having the child undergo psycho-educational assessment for learning difficulties and/or emotional/behavioural problems diagnosis can be complex and confusing process for a lot of parents as well as some teachers. Most parents do not know where to find clear information about psycho-educational testing, what the tests entail and how to understand and interpret the often complicated test scores. What is needed, therefore is to make the psycho-educational process as clear as possible for the benefit of parents and teachers

What is meant by psycho-educational testing has been explained earlier. Let me briefly explain the process again. Simply put, psycho-educational evaluation refers to psychological tests used by a duly certified or trained psychologist to analyse the mental processes that underlie a student's performance in school. Achievement and other tests may also be administered by the psychologist in the process.

There are so many psycho-educational tests available. Generally, the higher the validity and reliability coefficients of the tests, the better the tests are. Other factors such as ease of administration of the test, time it takes to administer the test, etc. may considered when selecting the tests to be used. A current version of Burrows Mental Measurement Year Book may help the psychologist to select appropriate tests for the psycho-educational evaluation. Briefly explained, validity refers to the question as to whether the test is measuring what it is supposed to measure while the term "reliability" implies whether the test is consistent. In view of the fact that these tests may be used to understand the nature and severity of the child's underlying disorders, it is absolutely important that teachers and parents should make every effort to understand what these tests mean.

Parents should make every effort to prepare the child for psycho-educational testing so as to reduce anxiety and encourage cooperation when the psychologist is administering battery of tests. One way to achieve such cooperation is for the parent to introduce discussion of the pending tests by the number of days as the child is old. For example, if the child is ten years old, the parent should discuss the subject with the child at least ten days in advance of the evaluation.

The parent should assure the child that the intent of the testing, that he or she is struggling in school in spite of efforts being made the teachers, the parent and the child for him/her to do well. Also, the parent should explain to the child that the tests will contain different types of questions, puzzles, drawings, and games; and that tests are not painful and it is not mean that he or she (the child) is crazy. Parents should reassure the child that the test will help find out as to how best he or she can be helped in school to succeed. Parent should respond to all questions that the child asks truthfully.

Parents should realize that the psychologist conducting the tests has been trained and certified/registered in his/her jurisdiction to manage children with a history of academic, behavioural/emotional difficulties, etc. Also, the psychologist do their very best to make children comfortable during testing. Parents should not expect their child to be aware of his/her performance. In order to maintain the integrity of the test, correct answers are not given to the child by the examiner. The most important thing is to make the examinee relax, comfortable and encouraged to him/her to make best effort.

The following suggestions are offered to parents and teachers:

Testing should be scheduled during the time of the day when the child functions best. Efforts should be made by the teacher to retain the child's classes or activities so that testing will not be a negative experience for the child. The child should be well rested and not hungry. If the parent decides to be at the school during the testing process he or she must plan to engage in some activity while the testing is in progress; and he/should not interfere with the testing in any way. Children normally feel better knowing that someone familiar is nearby while the testing is going on.

Generally, children will want to know about what is going to happen. The intent of the testing and the role of the psychologist conducting the tests should be clearly explained to the student. If the testing is to be conducted outside the school, it is suggested that the parent should visit the test site with the student before the first day of testing. When scheduling the testing session, the parent may try and find out about the expected type of questions, testing methods and the time it will take to complete each testing session. The examiner should explain to the parents and teachers all the student needs to know to complete testing successfully. It is also the role of the parent to take the child to the test site on time and in a state of mind that will enable the child to put forth his/her best effort during testing.

Observations of the child's behaviour during the sessions are important. For example, tests of skills increasingly present difficult problems or tasks until the child fails three or more. The psychologist will note the situation causing frustration, fatigue or delayed responses. This is all part of the psycho-educational evaluation process. The test administrator should encourage the child to do his or her best and not give up or be discouraged. Every effort should be made by the test administrator to get the child remain calm and comfortable during the testing. The psychologist should permit breaks when needed by the child.

Consideration for Psycho-educational Assessment

The most important question parent should ask themselves is when he/she should consider a psycho-educational evaluation for his/her the child. There are various ways by which the child could be tested,

School teachers or the school counsellor refer a child with learning and/emotional behaviour problems for testing. Sometimes parents themselves suspect that the child may be experiencing academic and/or emotional/behaviour problems. The parent then requests the school to have the child tested. Some parents think that their children have good or above average intelligence and do not understand or are frustrated as the why the child may be experiencing academic failures or unsatisfactory academic performance. In numerous instances, at times, both the parent and the teacher agree that the child works hard; and that something is wrong that is preventing the child from doing well. But they don't know what the problem is. There are also times when a teacher or a parent may be suspicious that the child's behaviour difficulties may stem from frustration resulting from his/her poor academic performance.

It should be noted that learning difficulties in school do not suddenly appear and may impact other areas. In fact, it is possible to trace the child's learning problems back several years. It makes sense for a parent to document what the parent may be observing over a period of time. This will enable the teacher and the parent to ascertain if there is a pattern of difficulty.

However, not all students with academic difficulties need to be given psycho-educational evaluation. Before psycho-educational evaluation may be considered, the parent and the teacher may work together to consider alternative learning strategies for the child. Based on the child's responses to these intervention strategies, the parent and the teacher can gain some insight as to whether or not formal psycho-educational assessment is warranted. Sometimes a little bit of help from the Resource Room teacher is all the child needs to overcome his/her specific learning issue. When the child continues to struggle with his school work despite the alternative intervention strategies and/or extra resource room assistance, then a neurologically-based learning disability may be considered, and the child may require thorough formal psycho-educational evaluation by a duly qualified or certified psychologist.

The following are some common academic problems children experience by children in school:

1. Poor attention span, and excessive daydreaming in class.
2. Poor concentration skills
3. Poor performance in one specific subject or area.
4. Difficulty in expressing thoughts in writing
5. Difficulty with math skills
6. Difficulty with short-term or long-term memory
7. Difficulty with speech.
8. Difficulty with receptive and/or expressive vocabulary.
9. Poor spelling skills
10. Poor comprehension skills
11. Unable to remember basic math facts.
12. Unable to sit still.
13. Poor organization skill
14. Difficulty finishing assignments or tests in the time allotted.
15. Poor performance despite working hard.
16. Class work is very messy or untidy.

In general, parents tend to have reservations about school's request to test their children. This may be attributed, in part, to negative experiences some parents may have had a child in school. Some tend to think that the test results may be reflection on their parenting skills or neglect. However, common concerns of parents include fear of having the child labelled; some are of the view that they may be pressured to have the child put on medication. Other parents demonstrate concern about negative stigma that may be attached to the child following diagnosis. Still in a lot of cases, the parent simply does have sufficient time to process the idea that the child is to be evaluated as a result of academic failure. Others need to know the intent and the nature of the assessment to be thoroughly explained in simple language and not the often confusing professional jargons.

Despite the reservations some parents may have about testing their child/children, tremendous benefit can be derived from the psycho-educational evaluation. For example, poor academic performance can impact the child's self-esteem as well as his/her relationship with friends and family. Many of these issues affecting the child can be addressed successfully if an assessment is conducted and appropriate intervention is identified and implemented.]

Severe Disabling Conditions.

In addition to some of the common academic problems described above some severe disabling conditions and definitions are adapted by many school jurisdictions. These include the followings:

1. Severe Cognitive Disability:

A student with severe mental disability is one who:

a) Has severe delays in all or most areas of development.

b) Frequently has other disabilities including physical, sensory, medical and/or behavioural.

c) Requires constant assistance and/or supervision in all areas of functioning including daily living skills and may require assistive technology.

d) Should have a standardized assessment which indicates functioning in the severe to profound range (standard score of 30+5 or less).. Functional assessments by a qualified professional will be considered in cases where the disabilities of the student preclude standardized assessment;

e) and has scores equivalent to the severe to profound level on an adaptive behavioural scale, e.g. AAMR

Adaptive Behavioural Scale or the Vineland Adaptive Behavior Scales, Scales of Independent Behaviour.

Note: Assessment by a Psychiatrist, Certified/Registered/ or Developmental Paediatrician or Registered Psychologist is required in nearly all jurisdictions in North America in all the cases described above.

2. **Severe Emotional/Behavioural Disability**

A student with a severe emotional/behavioural disorder is one who:

a) Displays chronic, extreme and pervasive behaviours which require close and constant adult supervision, high levels of structure, and other intensive support services in order to function in an educational setting. The behaviours significantly interfere with both the learning and safety of the student and other students; and

b) Has a diagnosis of psychosis including schizophrenia, bi-polar disorder, obsessive/compulsive disorders, or severe chronic clinical depression; and may display a self-abusive or aphasic behaviour and/or

c) Is dangerously aggressive, destructive, and has violent and impulsive behaviours toward self and/or others such as Conduct Disorder. In the most extreme and pervasive instances severe Oppositional Defiant Disorders may qualify.

A clinical diagnosis by a Psychiatrist, Certified/Register or Chartered Psychologist or developmental Paediatrician is required, in addition to extensive documentation of the nature, frequency, and severity of the disorder by the teacher and/or other school authorities. The effects of the disability on the student's functioning in the educational setting should be described. An ongoing treatment plan/behavioural plan should be available and efforts should be made to ensure that the student has access to appropriate mental health and therapeutic services.

3. Severe Multiple Disability.

A student with multiple disabilities is one who:

A).Has two or more non-associated moderate to severe cognitive and/or physical disabilities which, in combination, result in the student functioning at severe to profound level; and

b) Requires significant special programs, resources and/or therapeutic services.

Students with a severe disability with another associated disability is not designated under this category, but is designated under severe emotional/behavioural disability category.

In some school jurisdictions, the following mild or moderate disabilities cannot be used in combination with other disabilities to qualify under the severe disability category. These include:

1) Attention Deficit/Hyperactive Disorder (AD/HD)
2) Learning Disability (LD)
3) Emotional/Behavioural Disabilities.
4) Speech and Language Related Disabilities.

Severe Physical or Mental Disability – including Autism

A student with a severe physical, medical or neurological disability is one who:

a) Has a medical diagnosis of a physical disability, specific neurological disorder or medical condition which creates a significant impact on the student's ability to function in the school environment; and

b) Requires extensive adult assistance and modification to the learning environment in order in order to benefit from schooling.

A student with severe autism or other severe developmental disorder is included in this category. A clinical diagnosis by a psychiatrist, clinical psychologist, registered psychologist, or medical professional specializing in the field of autism is required.

In order for a diagnosis of autism to be made, the student needs to demonstrate difficulties in three broad areas:

a) Social interaction

b) Communication, or

c) Stereotyped pattern of behaviour (e.g. hand flapping, body rocking, echolalia; instances of sameness and resistance to change)..

A student diagnosed with severe Faetal Alcohol Spectrum Disorder (FASD) may have Faetal Alcohol Syndrome (FAS) or Alcohol-Related Neurological Disorder (ARND) and is included in this category. A clinical diagnosis by a psychiatrist, a certified psychologist with specialized training, or medical professional specializing in developmental disorders is required. Students with severe Faetal Alcohol Spectrum Disorder (FASD) who exhibit significant impairment in the areas of social functioning, life skills, behaviour, learning, attention and concentration, will need extensive intervention and support.

Deafness

A student with profound hearing loss is one who:

Has a hearing loss of 71 decibels (dB) or more unaided in the better ear over the normal speech range (500 and 4000 Hz) which interferes with the use of oral language as the primary form of communication, or has a cochlear implant preceded by a 71 dB hearing loss unaided in the better ear; and requires extensive modification and specialized educational support.

The student must be diagnosed by a clinical or educational audiologist.

Blindness

A student with a severe visual impairment is one who:

a) Has corrected vision so limited that it is inadequate for most or all instructional situations, and the information must be presented through other means; and

b) Has a visual acuity ranging from 6/60 (20/200) in the better eye after correction, to an angle of 20 degrees.

For those students who may be difficult to assess (e.g. cortical blindness – developmental delayed), a functional visual assessment by a qualified specialist in the field of vision or medical professional may be sufficient to suggest visual impairment.

Deciding to Have Your Child Tested

In the preceding paragraphs, I have indicated some of the reasons which may result in having a child referred for testing. It is also noted that while this book is focused on psycho-educational evaluation by a qualified psychologist, the student may also be needed to be tested by other professionals.

If a parent makes a decision to have that psycho-educational testing is likely to benefit his/her child, it makes sense for the parent to make an informed decision in choosing a psychologist. Generally, the School Counsellor and/or the Resource Room specialist at the child's school can guide the parent as to how to pursue the psycho-educational evaluation the school system.

School based assessments by a certified Psychologist can successfully identify a student with learning problems when the student is older and the academic failure is more pronounced. It is argued by some clinician that a school-based evaluation may miss subtle learning problems, particularly in bright children The writer does not share this opinion; if the psycho-educational assessment and is conducted by a well-trained and certified psychologist, then it makes no difference whether the testing is conducted in the school setting or by a private independent certified psychologist.

Parents should be aware that time can be a key concern when deciding to use a school-based psycho-educational evaluation. In view of the demands placed on the school-based psychologist, most often the assessment process in the school takes longer than using a private certified psychologist. However, using the services of a private psychologist can be very expensive. Generally, most school jurisdiction may not foot the bill of a private psychologist hired by the parent. Insurance is not likely to cover the expenses.

Also, the parent or guardian of the child may look into the time that may be spent evaluating his/her child. The time it may take to conduct the overall testing may depend upon the referral question; the hypothesis the psychologists may formulate as to what the child's problems may be and the kind of testing instruments the psychologist may decide to use to seek answers to the referral question. Thus, testing can take four hours to several days. Thus, psychologist should submit written report to the school, the parents or guardian with few days to few weeks after completion of the assessment.

A comprehensive evaluation should include a wide range of tests that can provide multi-layered view of the child's strengths and weaknesses. Typically, an evaluation may examine the child's cognitive ability; his or her academic achievement, and a number of more specific skills such as receptive and expressive language development, attention and concentration or developmental delays. A good psycho-educational evaluation report should help the parent/guardian, or the teacher understand exactly what skills are contributing the child's academic problems and how to strengthen those skills.

Whether the testing is school-based or conducted by a private certified Psychologist, a case conference involving the parent, teacher and the Psychologist should be held to explain the test results in a simple language that can be understood by the parent and the teacher. The case conference will be helpful in deciding what further steps should be taken. An IPP (Individual Program Plan) may be developed based on the test results and other relevant information about the child. Simply put the Psychologist and the parent along with the school personnel should work as a team to help alleviate the child's educational difficulties.

What Constitutes a Good Psycho educational Evaluation

A good psycho educational assessment comprises:

Referral question
Referral Source
Background Information
Assessment Procedures
Relevant Test Procedures
Assessment Results
Interpretation of Results
Summary and Recommendations

Referral Question:

It is imperative to identify the referral question. In other words, "why is the student referred for assessment? Psycho-educational assessments are conducted primarily to rule out a learning disability. What do we mean when we talk about the term "learning disability? One of the most commonly accepted definition of a learning disability is a "severe or very significant discrepancy between the child's cognitive ability and his or her achievement. However, there are other explanations as to why a child performs poorly in school, including attention problems, emotional problems, sub-average intelligence, such as borderline intellectual ability, and mental retardation. In some instances, the referral question may not be explicitly stated. Nevertheless, the referral question determines the specific areas to be included in the psycho educational evaluation.

Source of the Referral

The referral for the testing may be made by the teacher, the School Counsellor (with informed parental consent) or by the parent of the child.

Background Information

This include the child's educational history, current educational services or status, resource room test scores, results of any screening test, e.g. the Brisance Screening test. Family history in a least intrusive manner along with medical history will be helpful. The child's background information may also be obtained from discussion with the teacher, support staff, guidance counsellor.

Assessment Procedure

Here, the examiner should list all sources of information as well as all assessment procedures. These should include both formal and informal tests, questionnaires and any other testing the examiner may have conducted. Also, interviews, etc. should be listed.

As previously indicated assessment procedures are determined by the referral question and by the data gathered during assessment. In some cases, there are Provincial or State guidelines that must be adhered to when diagnosis learning disabilities.

Assessment for learning disabilities requires administration of the followings:

individually administered standardized intelligence test, such as the Wechsler Scales or Stanford Binet, Kaufmann Assessment Battery for Children.

individually administered achievement test with multiple measures of reading, mathematics, spelling, writing and possibly language, e.g. WRAT, WIAT, etc. latest editions.

additional cognitive testing in areas not addressed by the IQ tests, e.g. auditory/phonological processing, long-term retrieval and retention.

Moreover, if attention deficit/hyperactivity problems are indicated in the child's history, interview and/or assessment, additional evaluation must include rating scale to assess attention deficit/hyperactivity disorder and, if possible, include computerized test of attention, such as the TOVA or the Conner's Continuous Performance Scale. Finally, a measure of adaptive behaviour,, such as AAMD or the Vineland, must be included, if low borderline or mentally deficient intellectual functioning is suggested.

General Observation – Test Behaviour

Here information impacting rapport and the actual observations during the testing are reported. For example, the student's demeanour, work habits, motivation, energy level, attention span, concentration, mood, excessive talking, and other observed characteristics must be described in an objective, non-judgemental manner. Other unusual habits or mannerism should be described. Hearing or visual difficulties, wearing eyeglasses or contact lens or hearing aid should be indicated. Also, frequent requests by the client to have items repeated, requests for frequent breaks, handedness, etc. must be included in this section of the report.

Test Results

Results of testing are reported in terms of standard scores, percentile ranks and grade equivalents.

Standard Scores has predetermined mean of 100, and a standard deviation of 15. These scores can be added or subtracted for comparative purposes.

Percentile Score is a score that represents the person's rank, ranging from 1 to 99. For example, a percentile score of 60 suggests that the students score was equal to or better than 50 percent of the children in the standardization sample or whom the test was normed.

Grade Equivalents: In general, grade equivalents are rough approximation of the client's level of functioning is the area of an academic subject. Grade equivalents scores is average of the raw scores that were obtained by individuals in the nominative sample in a given grade. Grade equivalent scores can be misleading. For example, a Grade 3 student who obtains a grade equivalent score of 6.0 in math does not suggest that he or she can do grade 6 math. Rather, it simply means that the student in question did better than what is expected of students at his/her grade level. Thus, grade equivalent scores should be viewed with caution. A comparison of the standard score and the percentile ranks may give a better idea of the student's performance in a subject.

Interpretation of the Test Results.

The results of the test should be interpreted and integrated in a way that is meaningful to teachers, parents/guardians and to other readers. Global test scores (e.g., Full Scale IQ scores, composite scores on achievement tests) should preferably be discussed first with more specific information, such as composite or scale sores and individual subtest scores) to follow. The student's inter-individual strengths and weaknesses (i.e., his or her performance as compared to others in the standardization sample) as well as his/intra-individual strengths and weaknesses must be explained to the reader of the report.

As indicated earlier, a typical psycho-educational evaluation will look at the child's cognitive ability, academic achievement and a number of specific skills related to the learning process.

Intellectual Testing

The two tests of cognitive ability that are generally used by psychologists are the Wechsler scales, such as the Wechsler Intelligence Scale for Children IV Edition, the Wechsler Pre-School and Primary Scale of Intelligence and the Stanford-Binet Test of Cognitive Ability. These tests are used to determine a child's current level of intellectual functioning, "IQ."

Consider, for example, Mary's current level of overall intellectual functioning on the WISC-IV is in the High Average Range and exceeds those of approximately 84% of the children of her age group in the standardization sample (FSIQ = 115; 95 % Confidence Interval). What does this information actually mean? The statement implies that Mary Full Scale Intelligence of 115 places her in the percentile rank of 84th. The 84th percentile is considered to be within the High (Bright) Average range; and with 95% Confidence Interval, Mary true intellectual functioning is between 110 -120. Mary's IQ is equal to or better than 84% percent of the children of her age group on whom the test was standardized.

The Full Scale IQ

This comprises of a number of subtests on the WISC- IV grouped into four basic areas as follows:

Verbal Comprehension Index (VCI)

The VCI indicates the ability to use verbal skills gained through formal and informal education and exposure. This includes the ability to reason with words, to learn verbal material and to process verbal information. Children who have strong verbal skills generally do very well in the academic system, that those who have weak verbal skills.

Perceptual Reasoning Index (PRI)

The Perceptual Reasoning Index reflects the ability to reason with non-verbal information using skills such as fluid reasoning, non-verbal concept formation, visual perception and organization as well as visual motor coordination. These skills enable the individual to recognize patterns and to form mental pictures, which are critical in areas such as math word problems. Children who are strong in this area may be considered as more "intuitive" since they are able to solve problems, but not always able to describe how they arrive at the answer.

Working Memory Index (WMI)

The Working Memory Index (WMI) reflects the ability to pay attention to, and hold information in, one's mind long enough to use that information. Many things can impact on the individual's ability to remember things since memory is an extremely complex concept. This including attention, verbal abilities, organizational skills and retrieval skills (this involves the information getting in and locating that information once it is in there?).

Processing Speed Index (PSI)

The Processing Speed Index indicates the ability to mentally process routine information quickly and efficiently, without making many errors. These involve tasks that are generally assume to be automatic and do not need too much mental energy to perform, such as basic math fact. Many people may be considered as "bright" or "smart" but they work so slowly.

Academic Skills and Processing Issues

Assessment now focuses on the basic academic adjustment skills such as reading, spelling, and arithmetic as soon as the student's cognitive abilities have been determined. Other areas that contribute to the learning process are also examined. There are a many test batteries that may be used to determine the student's academic functioning. Most school jurisdictions use the "discrepancy model" for diagnosing a learning disability. This model suggests that there is a significant discrepancy or differences between the student's current level of intellectual functioning (IQ) and the child's academic performance, in one or more areas. There are numerous underlying skills that contribute to reading or math success. A thorough psycho-educational assessment should assist the parent and the teacher to uncover the specific skills the student may be struggling, and can benefit from intervention. In order to help the child successfully, it is critical the assessment helps to determine why the child is experiencing difficulties in a given subject area.

Basic Skills that must be Evaluated

These include the following: Phonetic awareness and decoding; Reading Comprehension; Attention; Fluency; Working Memory and Executive Functioning.

Phonetic Awareness and Decoding

This refers to the student's ability to associate a specific letter with the sound it makes. For example, remembering that the letter b makes a/b/ sound or the letters ch makes the /ch/ sound. This is one of the primary areas of difficulty in children with dyslexia. There are also children who have difficulty remembering the associations and therefore are unable to sound out an unfamiliar word when they see it (decoding). Other children have problem in distinguishing one sound form the other. These children have no phonetic awareness.

Reading Comprehension

Reading comprehension relates to the ability to understand, process and recall information that has been read. The underlying causes of poor reading comprehension may be determined by administering a test that requires the student to read aloud. When the difficulties in reading comprehension relates to a weakness in the student's ability to decode words, he or she may read slowly, stumble over words or substitute words that appear similar. Also, poor reading comprehension may be indicative of the student's failure to process and store what he or she reads. At times, this may be due to "inattention". A child with Attention Deficit Hyperactive Disorder (ADHD) may not be able to answer question about what he or she has read. This is due to the fact that the child has not processed the material in a way that enables him or her to remember and recall it.

Attention

Attention refers to a term that incorporates a number of skills. There are number of ways by which to evaluate attention. These include tests such as the Attention Deficit Disorder Evaluation Scale which is a parent teacher checklists, formal tests given by the psychologist, some computerized tests such as the Test of Variable of Attention (TOVA) or the Conner's Continuous Performance Test, and a standardized developmental history. Sometimes, a parent will report that his/he child is easily distracted or the child does not seem to listen. However, it must be noted that a number of things, such as emotional issues, can interfere with the child's attention. A child with Attention Deficit Hyperactive Disorder (ADHD) is likely to have problems across many issues in addition.

Fluency

This implies the speed with which the student can perform a task accurately that should be automatic. In general, these tasks do not use a great deal of mental energy, e.g., recalling single digit math facts or reading short sentences. Some students have the necessary academic skills to perform the task, but perform the task at a very slow pace. Such students hardly seem to complete their tasks in the time allotted. Giving such students extended time to finish their work is helpful and may boost their self-esteem. Students with Attention Deficit Hyperactive Disorder (ADHD) often have difficulty with time management; they are unable to keep of the passage of time when working. As a result, they run out of time. Such student may benefit from extra time along with imposed external structure on the extra time.

Working Memory

This refers to the individual' ability to remember information long enough to make use of it. Memory challenges involve encoding, storage and retrieval. Encoding implies the initial perception and registration of information. Storage is the retention of the encoded information over a period of time. Retrieval, on the other hand, refers to the process of using stored information. To successfully recall a student's prior experience, he or she first encodes, stores and then retrieves information about that particular experience. On the other hand, memory failure or forgetting an important fact suggests a breakdown in one of these stages of memory.

One must note the difference between working memory and long term-memory. Long-term memory has to do with information that one has been learnt or acquired over a period of time. Working memory has to do with information that one "juggles" in one's mind as the individual attempts to do something with that information. For example, is when the individual remember a telephone number for a long period of time and then try to dials the number. As pointer out earlier, memory is one of the most complex processes of functioning which can be impacted by a number of processing disorders.

Executive Functioning

The term, Executive Functioning deals with the individual's ability to organize information in such a way that that enables him or her to achieve a particular goal in future. A number of skills come under the general umbrella of executive functioning. These include planning and organization, time management, working memory, emotional regulations, self-monitoring and the ability to inhibit one's impulses. These skills are dependent on maturation in specific areas of the brain. This implies that until those areas are developed, it is difficult for the child to perform tasks that require the development of strong executive functioning. The brain of the child continues to develop to his/her 20s. There are indications to suggest that children with Attention Deficit Hyperactive Disorder show much slower development in the areas of the brain that relates to executive functioning. Some experts have suggested that the brain development of a child with ADHD is about 30 percent slower than their peers. This means that a 10-year old chid with ADHD may really be functioning at the level of a typical 7-years old, which suggests executive functioning is one of the key deficits for children with ADHD. Some students with ADHD are able to compensate for their ADHD in the elementary school. However, they start to stumble in middle school when the demands on executive functioning significantly increase.

Next, the Psychologist may be interested in the student's language development. He/she may use the Peabody Picture Vocabulary Test and the Expressive One Word Picture Vocabulary Test to determine Receptive and Expressive language development. Low scores on these tests may suggest delayed language development. The Psychologist may recommend intervention by a Speech-Language Pathologist.

To determine the student's current functioning in the three areas of school adjustment (Reading, Spelling and Arithmetic), the Psychologist may administer the WRAT or the WIAT to the student. The Woodcock Reading Mastery Test mayadminister to determine the child's reading comprehension skills.

For auditory processing problem, the Psychologist may use such tests as Wepman Auditory Discrimination Test and the Goodman Fristoe Test of Auditory Discrimination. Poor performance on these tests of auditory acuity may result in a referral to an audiologist and/ or physician for further diagnosis and therapeutic intervention, if necessary.

Next, the Psychologist may administer the Bender Visual-Motor Gestalt Test and the Benton Test of Visual-Motor Integration to the student. Unsatisfactory performances may suggest visual-motor co-ordination and visual-motor integration problems. Referral for therapeutic intervention may be made to a physician and/or an ophthalmologist.

If the referral also indicates an emotional/behaviour problems, the psychologist uses such test as the Emotional/Behaviour Identification Scale and the Behaviour Disorders Identification Scale, both HOME and SCHOOL versions to gather information about the student. The psychologist may observe the student's behaviour, and may conduct clinical interviews with the teacher and the student to gather additional information.

Where personality issues are suggested, the Psychologist may use the Personality Inventory for Children or the Adolescent Psychopathology Scale to aid in the diagnosis and intervention.

If Attention Deficit Hyperactive (ADD/ADHD) is suspected, the Psychologist may use the Attention Deficit Disorder Evaluation Scale (Home and School Versions to gather data that may helpful in referral and treatment. Other computerized assessment instruments such as the Conner's Continuous Performance Test and/or the Tests of Variable of Attention (TOVA) may be employed.

Teachers and parents must note that there are many other psycho-educational instruments that the psychologist may choose, at his/her discretion, to respond to the referral question (s).

Summary and Recommendations

The Summary and Recommendations is arguably the most important part of the report. It is unfortunately this area where some psycho-educational reports tend to fall short. Well trained and experienced psychologists should be able to produce well-founded recommendations, especially instructional recommendations. A concise summary of the most relevant background and assessment results should be followed by clearly stated diagnosis. This should be followed by specific instructional strategies. Educationally relevant suggestions should be obtained from the assessment data. In addition to educational recommendations, recommendations for referrals to other professionals such as an audiologist or ophthalmologist, or clinical psychologist, psychotherapist etc. may be made. These recommendations must be appropriate and relevant.

Educational Recommendations

Also, educational recommendation is an important aspect of the psycho-educational assessment report; and must be relevant for educational programming for the child. The well trained and experienced psychologist interprets the assessment data and makes research-based recommendations.

Case Conference after the Diagnosis

The results of psycho-educational assessment can be very complicated. Thus, parents and teachers often need time to read the assessment report more than once, and digest the information. Sometimes parents and teachers do not thoroughly understand the report in view of the professional terms and jargons used. Some parents can become confused or sad when they read the report and cannot believe what is said in the report.

In some cases, the diagnosis may actually bring satisfaction and relief rather than grief. It is strongly recommended a case conference involving the psychologist, the parent and/or the teachers be held to explain the report. This will enable the parent and the teachers to ask questions they do not understand in the psycho-educational evaluation report. Hopefully, the case conference will enable the psychologist, the parent and the teaching staff to decide jointly as to what further steps should be taken to help the child. The diagnosis of the child's learning difficulties ends speculations for parents and teachers. It is recommended that the child should be re-evaluated every three years. Current report findings are necessary to help determine whether the child can continue to be eligible for special services.

Some of Parental Concerns following the Evaluation

Let us consider some common questions ask

How come my child's scores on the reading test were in the average range, but not as strong as her cognitive abilities indicate. Is my child learning disabled?

There are some in educational psychology professionals who view the term learning disability as a significant discrepancy between the student's overall intellectual functioning (Full Scale IQ) and his or her performance in reading or the child's specific reading skills is significantly below average. A number of schools tend to use the discrepancy model. However, there must be evidence to suggest that the weakness is creating impairment in the child's school functioning. Thus, it is not sufficient to demonstrate that the child is not performing at a level that is consistent with his or her potential.

In the case of the second definition, however, a significant discrepancy would suggest a weakness if the student's skills were within the average range, but it would not necessarily imply or suggest a reading disability such as dyslexia. Most professional would probably agree that a child with learning disability would show difficulty across several language-based tests which may lead to impairment in his or her school functioning.

The Parent will want to know what next steps should be taken. Now, what do I do with results of the evaluation?.

Hopefully, the case conference would have helped to clarify the child's test results. The parent or guardian or the student and the teachers may have had their concerns of the test results addressed during the case conference with the psychologist. A review of the evaluation will indicate or help determine how the student's weaknesses may be causing impairment in his or her learning. A number of accommodation or interventions can be implemented and/or support services provided, based on the test finding and the psychologist's recommendations.

The Parent may also wants to if the child will continue to have this problem.

The answer to this question is not that simple. This is because the child's brain continues to develop. Extra help such as coaching or tutoring can help; however, some residual effects may continue to be evident if the child is re-tested as an adult. In most cases, children with reading disorders learn to read reasonably well enough to meet demands of life, though they may read more slowly and are likely to be poor spellers. Children with Attention Deficit Hyperactive Disorder (ADHD) generally tend to outgrow hyperactivity as their brain develops. They are likely to perform executive functions in adulthood. Nevertheless, they are likely to continue to need to perform much harder than someone who has no ADHD.

REFERENCES

Bermudez and Ralow. Psychometric View of Culture and Context: Research on Test Bias. National Research Council, 1982

Blac. Intelligence Test of Cultural Homogeneity: Assessment of Intellectual Functioning. BITCH 100. Wikipedia

Graham, John; Nuglien, Jack A. Hanbook of Psychological Assessment. Google Books. ISBN:1264512, 2003

Graham, John R & Lilly, Roy S. Psychological Testing. Englewood Cliffs, New Jersey: Prentice- Hall, 1984

Lyon, G. R (1996). Learning Disabilities, reprinted in 98/99 Annual Editions: Educating Exceptional Children, Freiburg, K.L., ed. Guilford, CT: Dushkin/McGraw-Hill

Harrell, J.P. Physiological Responses to Racism and Discrimination. NRC: PubMed Central, 2003.

Mather, N. (1999). Interpretations of WJ-R cognitive and achievement batteries. Presentation to Knox County School, October, 1999.

Mather, N. & Jaffe, L.E (1992). Woodcock-Johnson Psycho educational Battery-Revised: Reports and Recommendations. (New York: Wiley.

Mather, N, et al. The Woodcock-Johnson III Tests of Cognitive Ability and Tests of Achievement. National Association of School Psychologists, April, 2001.

McGrew, K.S & Woodcock, R. Woodcock-Johnson III technical Manual. Chicago: Riverside Publishing, 2001.

Mensah, Joseph A. Multiculturalism and the Education System. Journal of Education. Halifax: Nova Scotia Dept. of Education,, Vol.15.No1, 1978.

Overton, T. Assessment in Special Education: An Applied Approach, 3rd ed. Upper River, NJ: Prentice Hall, 2000

Reynolds, Cecil; Suzuki,Lisa. Bias in Psychological Assessment: An Imperial Review and Recommendation: PSOF, 2003.

Reynolds, Cecil; Ramsay. Understanding in Psychological Assessment: Minority Objection to the Test Bias, PSOF, 2003

West, T. et al. Cultural Diversity and Ethnic Minority Psychology: Student Publication. York, 2016:

Williams, A. Assessing Children's Implicit Attitudes Using Affective Misattribution. Journal of Cognition and Personality Dev. 17:505-525, 2016 Stern, Begg. Alternative Approaches to Assessment, NAP. EDS, 1995

CHAPTER II

BEHAVIOUR DISORDERS IN SCHOOLS

In the first chapter, the writer has discussed the Psycho-educational process at length, including some of the instruments used in the assessments and the identification or children at risk and those with emotional and behaviour disorders. Similar instruments may be used by a trained and certified/registered psychologist or the educational psychologists in the assessment and the identification of gifted and talented students. Other forms of assessments in the school systems include Speech and Language, Medical, Dental, etc. Those types of assessments and treatments will left to the trained experts in those fields.

This chapter will focus on further identification, assessment and correction of behaviour disorders in schools.

All teachers in the school systems regardless of whether they teach in the regular classroom, mainstream, integrated or special education will, come across students with behaviour disorders. Generally, behaviour disorders take place within the interaction between the student and his/her environment. Behaviour disorders result from conflict with the environment.

Behaviour disorders vary in type and in severity, ranging from the mildly disruptive behaviours which can be infuriating to some people, to the severely disruptive, which can be physically violent. Irrespective of the nature of a specific behaviour disorder, the classroom teacher must be prepared and able to play a significant role in the correction of the behaviour disorders so that all his/her student can benefit from his/her teaching as much as possible.

In order to maximize the benefits of the educational experience for all the students, the classroom teacher plays a pivotal role in the identification, assessment, and correction of behaviour disorders. Typically, the ultimate correction of a behaviour disorder involve the cooperation of teachers, the student, and other professionals, yet it remains the primary responsibility of the classroom teacher to integrate a variety of perspectives stemming from the participation of others into a realistic plan and implementation of the corrective strategy. In fulfilling their role responsibilities, it is important to recognize from the very beginning that there are no simple, ready-made solutions to a behaviour disorder situations and that there seem to be a constant interplay of both objective and subjective factors.

We may note, for example, that the identification and assessment of behaviour disorders, is both an objective and subjective process. It is objective based on the observable and measureable characteristics of the specific behaviour, and of its consequences on the educational process. Moreover, assessments are subjectively based on the values of each teacher and perceptions as to what constitutes acceptable and unacceptable behaviour in his or her classroom. In addition, a choice of strategy for the correction of a behaviour disorder is likely to vary as a function of the teacher's training, value system, experience, and the availability of additional resources.

In view of the variability of behaviour disorders both in type and severity, as well as the variability of the teacher characteristics a broad range of behaviour disorders is addressed by the writer. It is the author's primary objective to present a basic and very practical document for parents, school administrators, and the classroom teacher, who in addition to providing education instruction in the classroom, is also the most important agent for the identification, prevention, assessment and correction of behaviour disorders in the classroom. The second objective is to provide some practical framework on behaviour disorders which can serve as supplement to the existing working relationship between, the parents, students, resource personnel, administrators and the classroom teacher.

In order to achieve these objectives, the writer focuses on the conceptual objectives that behaviour disorders arise out of the situations where there is a conflict between the student and the educational process the effects of which minimizes the benefits students can derive from the educational experience. A single definition of a behaviour disorder has limited functional use for the classroom teacher due to the variation in type and severity of behaviour disorders.

Instead, behaviour disorders are functionally defined along a continuum based on the degree to which they disrupt the educational process. Thus, the writer view behaviour disorders as encompassing, does not specify, traditional definitions of, for example, "emotional disturbance", "social maladjustment", "conduct disorder", etc., The primary reason for opting for more generic approach in this chapter is that a continuum of behaviour disorders has four distinct categories.

Provide for functional definition of behaviour disorders based on the situation, inclusive of both objective and subjective factors; it directly facilitates the identification of behaviour disorders; it provides a practical framework for the assessment of behaviour disorders; it gives a practical framework for the selection and development of corrective teaching strategies.

Definition of Behaviour Disorders

A definition of behaviour disorders may suggest two main factors. The first is an understanding or a perspective on why humans behave the way they do, and the reason for providing the definition, As an educator, and a trained educational psychologist, the behaviour which occurs in the classroom is of primary interest to the writer, although arguably the same general principles, would hold in other environments. Regarding an educational perspective on the definition emphasis will be on those situations that results from the students' interaction with the educational environment and process, the effects of which limits the benefits the students derive their educational experience.

There are many and complex factors that contribute a behaviour disorder. These range from the characteristic of the people involved, to the characteristics of the educational environment. Students are likely to act and react in unique ways in different situations, since they are unique individuals. Also, teachers, school counsellors, parents, school administrators and resource personnel, are unique individuals, and also likely to act and react differently depending on the circumstances. Thus, the characteristics of all these unique individuals will play a significant role in a behaviour disorder, since these individuals interact with each other in the context of the educational process.

One should not overlook the characteristics of the environment, such rules, routines, physical structure, and performance expectations in any behaviour. Thus, behaviour disorder as viewed by the writer is defined in a practical manner and expressed in terms of the number of situational characteristics, which when present in sufficient degree, disrupts or have negative impact on the educational process.

By defining behaviour disorder this way, a functional definition is presented, which also, reflects the purpose. This suggests that behaviour disorder is defined in a practical manner so as to enable the classroom teacher to arrive at best possible informed decisions concerning. identification, assessment and correction of the disordered behaviour or situation.

Moreover, behaviour disorders are defined along a continuum since teachers face many problems in their classroom which may not, on the surface appear severely disruptive but which, if ignored could escalate to a point where they may be very costly to the teacher and the student. The advantages of such a definition are based on the assumption that, being functional and broadly based, the definition corresponds directly to the situation at hand. This implies that the teacher and others who may be associated not only define behaviour disorders based on their experiences, but also construct a functional framework for making informed decision in regards to identification, assessment and correction at the same time.

In the schools, a behaviour disorder takes place when students respond to the educational environment in ways that significantly deviates from age-appropriate expectations, and which interfere with their own learning as well as others. Behaviour disorder is viewed along a continuum since all students exhibit demonstrate inappropriate behaviour at some time in some places

One end of the continuum represents situations within which students exhibit such behaviours infrequently and briefly, in relatively few settings to a mild degree. The other end of the continuum represents a much smaller of situations within which students exhibit such behaviour with high frequency, for extended period of time, in many situations, and to an extreme degree.

The teacher may conclude that as the level of the severity of the behaviour disorder increases, so should the extent and the nature of the intervention or corrective strategy. Mild behaviour disorders may best be corrected in the regular classroom setting, with support to the family and the teacher as may be necessary. Other measures may be required as the level of the severity of the behaviour disorder increases. Such measures include resource personnel, behavioural aides, clinical and residential classes, as well as special classes. The required interventions in situations of mild behaviour disorder may be informal and brief. However, in situations of severe behaviour disorder, intervention can be expected to be both intensive and prolonged,

The severity of a behaviour disorder is judged in terms of its effects on the education of the student rather than being based strictly on the characteristics of the particular behaviour. Due to the many subjectivity factors in the definition and the identification, a precise standard definition of the "Mild," "Moderate", and "Severe" is not possible. However, what is possible is the provision of examples of each of each degree or level to assist teachers in making their own decision. The severity of a behaviour disorder may be considered in terms of characteristics, which either individually or in various combinations, typically characterize behaviour disorders.

These characteristics are:

the demonstration of instability to establish or maintain satisfactory relationships with peers or adults;

the demonstration of general mood of unhappiness or depression;

the demonstration of inappropriate behaviour or feelings under ordinary conditions;

the demonstration of a continued difficulty in coping with the learning situation in spite of remedial intervention;

the demonstration of physical symptoms or fear associated with personal or school issues;

the demonstration of difficulties in accepting the realities of personal responsibilities and accountability.

In the preceding, the writer has discussed behaviour disorder from a generalized perspective. To facilitate the process of identification, assessment and correction of behaviour disorders, it is essential to complement this generalized perspective with description of any behaviour. Ii must be emphasized that all behaviour whether positive or problematic, can be analyzed in terms of seven observable dimensions which include 1context, 2.complexity, 3.directionality, 4.intensity, 5. frequency, 6. duration, 7. consistency.

The key to identifying, assessing and correcting a behaviour disorder is the analysis of the behaviour disorder in terms the seven dimensions previously discussed. A description of these seven dimensions are as follows:

Context. Context may be viewed as the relationship of the behaviour disorder to the ongoing process of environmental events. Context may be specifically defined in terms of the behaviour events which provide and follow specified behaviours which constitute the behaviour disorder. This implies that context identifies and defines the antecedents of the behaviour which is producing the disruption, and the consequences of the behaviour in the environment.

Complexity: This refers to the variety of the specific behaviours which are observed to be part of the behaviour disorder. Some behaviour disorders are simple in that there is but a single specific behaviour which requires correction. The corrective program, therefore, would be developed to reduce or eliminate the behaviour. The fact that there is one behaviour only does not necessarily imply the behaviour disorder would be defined as mild.

Depending on its other dimensions, a single behaviour such as poking with a sharp object could be defined as severe. Behaviour disorders become more difficult to deal with as complexity increases. The various components of the behaviour disorder would have to be priorized in terms of developing an overall corrective strategy.

Directionality: The directionality of the behaviour refers to those individuals affected by the behaviour. Individuals affected may be a student, the teacher and other students. A situation can be collectively more severe. For example, the escalation of disruptive behaviour can lead to a tense classroom atmosphere where once harmony and peacefulness existed.

Corrective strategies will vary as the directionality of the behaviour disorder varies. Where other students are affected and involved, they may have to be taught how to respond to the inappropriate behaviour as part of the corrective strategy. Likewise, as the behaviour disorder involves the interaction between the student and teacher, changes in the teacher's behaviour will have to be given serious consideration.

Intensity: Intensity may be defined in terms of how disturbing a particular behaviour is. While intensity is in part a quantitative dimension of behaviour, e.g. how loudly a student argues with the teacher, it is also to a large degree qualitative and subjective. For example, it will be difficult to measure how loudly a student argues.. In lieu of a quantitative measure of intensity, it is possible to qualitatively distinguish between arguing in a normal, raised, or screaming voice. Similarly, a student's poking behaviour may be characterized or defined as aggravating, annoying or hurtful.

Thus, the definition of intensity is particularly susceptible to the subjective perception of the teacher. If the teacher is having a particular good day, behaviour disorders are more likely to be viewed as less intense due to the teacher's greater degree of tolerance. The same behaviour at a different time or in a different classroom with a different teacher may be viewedas more intense or disturbing. Some teachers structure the classroom so that so that students are encouraged to argue rationally, and even a raised voice is often reinforced for its demonstration of student commitment to a point of view.

Other teachers structure their classrooms with much stricter rules about the questioning of rules, regulations and authority. While most students can adjust to the varying demands and expectations of different teachers at different time, students who are vulnerable to behavioural disorders experience have considerable difficulty when expectations vary and change without clear explanation. Intensity as well as other dimensions of a behaviour disorder, therefore, is much a product of teacher s as it is of student characteristics.

Consistency: Consistency refers to how typical the behaviour disorder is in totality of the student's experience, particularly in terms of the number and types of different environments in which the behaviour occurs. A functional definition will indicate whether the behaviour disorder occurs in one particular classroom, in all classrooms, on the school grounds, in the community at large and/or in the home. The strategies for assessment and correction will vary as a function of the consistency of the behaviour disorder simply because more people will have to be involved. A general rule is that the more consistent or pervasive a behaviour disorder is, the more structured assessment and correction will have to be.

Frequency: Frequency is simply how often a specific behaviour occurs, and if the behaviour is operationally defined, ie. defined in terms of which allow for direct measurement, frequency can be measured as easily by a variety of methods. In the identification of a behaviour disorder, however, statements about frequency can be misleading, particularly if they are not operationally defined.

Duration Duration is a measure of how long each episode of the behaviour may last. Duration may be short. Poking some one, for example, may last only one second per episode because it may be a single jab in the tigh of a student sitting next to the offender. On the other hand, the duration per episode may be longer, as in the case where poking is defined as a series of multiple jabs in rapid succession until the other student cries out in pain or annoyance. In each instance, the selection of a corrective strategy may be different. Another example of duration may be considered in a situation where a teacher identifies the problem subjectively.

Identification, Assessment, and Program Planning for the Behaviourally Disordred Child.

The earlier discussion of behaviour was aimed at providing a framework for the functional identification of behaviour disorders. The identification process itself involves two steps. First, the teacher needs a strategy for the initial clarification and definition of a situation which he or she has become aware of and is concerned about it. Consideration of the seven dimension of behaviour disorder will facilitate the teacher's definition of the situation in terms of its potential for formal assessment and intervention.

It may occur that, during this first step, the teacher recognizes the potential for escalation and, and without formal procedures, is able to take preventive or corrective action. It may also be the case that that this first step will result in a 'red flag", a caution for the teacher to be alert for repeated episode and escalation.. While conducting an identification process, it should be noted that one negative episode does not constitute a behaviour disorder..

The next step in the identification process requires the teacher to make a decision whether or not to proceed with a formal assessment, the fact remains that a formal assessment is time consuming, and that resources to conduct an assessment are often in high demand and in short supply.

To assist the teacher conduct an identification process, including using his or her judgement as to whether a formal assessment is called for, an identification checklist may be helpful

Assessment:, The process of assessment, program planning and evaluation are closely related and, for this reason, are considered jointly in this section. Assessment may be defined as the process of gathering information and stating what the problem is; Program planning, on the other hand, is specifying how the problem can be corrected; while evaluation is the process of determining the effect, or impact, of the corrective strategy. The eventual program plan depends on the methods used to assess. In view of these interdependencies, the process of assessment is critical.

As in the process of identification, assessment involves both objective data as well as subjective perceptions and impressions. Also, assessment is based on an analysis of the seven dimensions of behaviour discussed earlier. The primary difference between assessment and identification is that assessment is more formalized, structured and systematic.

The purpose of an assessment is to gain specific information about the student and his or her situation in order to facilitate informed decision making by those sharing responsibility for corrective measures. The assessment process will vary as the relative severity of the behaviour disorder varies. For mild behaviour disorders, assessment may be relatively informal and limited in scope, based on those obvious dimensions of which the teacher readily identifies as the key the problem.

In these instances, the need for documentation may be minimal since these instances are those which occur infrequently in any classroom. On the other hand, if behaviour disorders are more severe, the process of assessment will be more formal and extensive and will require documentation. The point is that informed decision-making is often a matter of good common sense with mild behaviour disorders, but usually a rigorous and challenging task in severe cases.

One objective of an assessment is to enable the development of a functional plan for correction which would: 1), identify the specifics of the behaviour disorder in terms of the dimensions of behaviour; 2), efficiently communicate the information about the behaviour disorder in terms of the seven dimensions of behaviour and, 3).specify the corrective strategy.

A second objective of the assessment is to provide a framework is to provide framework for the evaluation of the corrective strategy. This implies that method used to assess the behaviour disorder would also be used to determine the effect of the corrective strategy.

Consistent with the definition of behaviour disorder previously discussed, a functional framework for the assessment of behaviour disorders is based on the rational that:

1.behaviour disorders exist within the interaction between the student and his or her educational environment, and are the result of conflict between the student and his or her educational environment. Conflict is defined as the product of opposing sets of behavioural standards and/or expectations;

2. corrective strategies will focus on the student as well as the student's environment, which may include classroom, the school, the community at large, and/or the home; and

3.correction of the behaviour disorder will be achieved by changing the student, changing aspects of the environment or, in most instances, changing both to a certain degree. Environment is defined as all the persons, objects and events existing together in time and space.

REFERENCES

Axelrod, Behaviour Identificaton for the Classroom Teacher, New York: McGraw-Hill, 1977

Bernstein, G.S, et al. Behaviour Habilitation Through Proactive Programming. Baltimore, Md.:Brookes, 1981.

Bernstein, G.S.et al. Behavioural Rehabilitation Through Proactive Programming. Baltimore, Md: Brookes, 1981.

Bradley, R.K.et al. A national perspective on Children with Emotional disorders, Behaviour Disorders. 29:211-233, 2004

Cartwright, C.A., and Cartwright, G.P. Developing Observation Skills. New York: McGraw-Hill, 1974.

Clarizio, H.F and McCoy, G..M. Behaviour Disorders in Chiildren (2nd edi.).Nwe York: Crowell, 1976.

Colvin, Geoff. Diffusing Disruptive Behaviour in the Classroom. Thomsand Oaks: Corwin, 2010.

Crinmins, Daniel B. Positive Strategies for Students with Problems. Baltimore, MD: Brookes, 2007.

Csapo, M. Children With Behaviour and Social Disorders. A Canadian Focus, Vancouver, B.C, Center For Human Development and Research, 1981.

Cutela, J.R. Behaviour Analysis Forms for Clinical Intervention. Champaign, Ill.: Research Press. 1977.

Dreikurs, R. Psychology in the Classroom: A Manual for Teacher (2nd. ed.). New York: Harper and Row, 1968.

Ellis, A, Wolfe, J.L, and Mosley, S. How to raise an Emotionally Healthy, Happy Child. Hollywood, C.A.:Wilshire, 1974.

Egger, H.L, R. Angold. Emotional and Behaviour Disorders in Pre-School Children. Journal of Child Psychology and Psychiatry. 47:313-337, 2006.

Flanders,, N. Analyzing Teacher Behaviour. Menlo Park. Calif.: Addison-Wesley, 1970.

Hanmill, D.D; Bartel, N.R and Bunch, G.O. Teaching Children with Learning and Behaviour Problems. (Canadian Edition), Toronto. Ont.: Allyn and Bacon, 1984.

Kendall, P.C.and Norton-Ford, J.D.: Clinical Psychology: Scientific and Professional Dimensions. New York: John-Wiley, 1982.

Kessler, J.W. Psychopathology of Childhood. Englewood Cliffs. N.J: Prentice-Hall, 1966.

Kauffman, J.M., et al. Problems related to Under service os Students with Emotional or Behaviour Disorders. Behaviour Disorders. 43: 47-57, 2007.

Landrum, T.J, et al. What is Special Education for Students with Emotional or Behaviour Disorders. Journal of Special Education. 37:148-156, 2006.

Losen, M.., and Diament, B. Parent Conferences in Schools. Boston: Allyn and Bacon, 1978.

Mah, Ronald. Behaviour in Early Childhood Thomsand, CA: Corwin Press, 2007

McCallon, E., and McGray, E. Planning and Conducting Interviews. Austin, Texas: Learning Concepts, 1975.

Newcomer, P.L Understanding and Teaching Emotionally Disturbed Children. Boston, Mass.: Allyn Bacon, 1980.

One Giant Step: The Integration of Children with Special Needs. Program 10: The Behaviourally Disordered, Alberta Education, 1983

Osborne, Allan, et al, Discipline in Special Education. Thomsand Oaks, CA: Corwin Press, 2009.

Simonson, L.R. A Curriculum Model for Individuals with Severe Learning and Behaviour Disorders. Baltimore, Md.: University Park Press, 1979.

Stephens, L.R. Hartman, A.C.and Lucas, V.H. Teaching Basic Skills: A Curriculum Handbook. Columbus, Ohio Charles E. Merrill, 1978.

CHAPTER III

CORRECTIVE STRATEGIES FOR BEHAVIOUR DISORDERS IN SCHOOL

The primary objective of this chapter is to outline a number of preventive, as well as corrective, strategies which can be used in the classroom, and to advise on the selection of the most appropriate strategy for the identified behaviour disorder. In order to meet this objective, this chapter is organized into for parts:1) Prevention Strategies; (2) Strategies for Mild Behaviour Disorders; (3) Strategies for Severe Behaviour Disorders; and (4) Suggestions for Strategy Selection.

The preventive strategies are of two kinds. First, many of them can be incorporated into the teacher's natural style in the classroom. in an unstructured fashion, while others are specific types of structured activities the teacher can use to develop the coping and problem solving skills of the students. The strategies for mild behaviour disorders can also, to a large extent, be used naturally by the teacher, but are more likely to be focused on specific behaviour disorders of specific students. The strategies for severe behaviour disorders are those which are highly structured in their application, required documentation, and in some instances, involve aversive consequences for inappropriate behaviour. Finally, in those instanes where the behaviour disorder is rated, the teacher will have to use his or her judgement in selecting the most appropriate strategy from those presented for both mild and severe behaviour disorders.

Prevention: Undoubtedly the best approach to behaviour disorders in the schools is to prevent them from occurring in the first place. This may be easier said than done, but the fact remains that teachers can take many positive steps during the course of their natural activities which can help themselves and their students avoid the costly disruptions brought on by behaviour problems. The objective here is to define what is meant by 'prevention," to provide a framework for preventive strategies, and to indicate some specific techniques that can be used in their classrooms.

The term "prevention" can be confusing in that it is used to denote many different concepts and strategies. A generally accepted clarification was first proposed by Caplan (1961) who defined three qualitatively different preventive strategies: primary, secondary, and tertiary. The tertiary prevention refers to strategies aimed at reducing the residual effects of a chronic, or long-term disorder. Secondary prevention involves the identification of disorder as well as strategies to keep these disorders from escalating to severe and disruptive levels. Both tertiary and secondary prevention address disorders that already exist. Primary prevention here, has as its objective the reduction in the incidence of behaviour disorders, that is, the reduction of the number of new instances of behaviour disorder.

The likelihood that a behaviour disorder will occur may be viewed as the combined influence of several negative and positive factors. Negative factors which increase a student's risk for a behaviour disorder are:

1. Genetic, biological and physical abnormalities or injuries;

2. life crisis events, e.g., death in the family, separation/divorce of parents.

3. Environmental stressors (situations or conditions for which the student does not have an"automatic' response available.

Positive factors which decrease a student's risk of behaviour disorder include:

1. The existence of healthy support systems, eg. family, peers;

2. Social competence, e.g., problem solving skills. Interpersonal skills.

There are two basic approaches that teachers can use in the classroom to reduce the incidence of behaviour disorders. First, teachers can reduce stressful factors which may precipitate a behaviour disorder. A teacher blushes a number of classroom routines to increase predictability and clarity of expectations is reducing potential stress and, therefore, engaging in primary prevention. The second approach teachers can take is to increase the students' abilities to deal more effectively with problem situations. For example, the teacher who holds classroom meetings to facilitate students solving their own problems, is teaching students how to problem-solve, therefore promoting their ability and competence to deal with other problems in the future.

As can be seen from these examples, the focus of primary prevention is on the antecedents of behaviour. Students who are vulnerable to behaviour disorders, i.e., students who are most susceptible to stress or who have weaker coping skills, are particularly vulnerable to a number of hazards in the classroom environment. The following conditions and situations represent the most significant risks for students in terms of increasing the chances of behaviour disorder occurring:

L unstructured activities;

2 transition time between activities or classes;
3 inconsistent use of rewards and punishment by teachers;
4 frustrating or boring academic tasks;
5 competitive games and/or activities;
6 unpredictable teacher reactions;
7 highly stimulating environments and activities; and
8 delays and interruptions in classroom routines or activities.

The teacher who structures his or her classroom and instructional environment to avoid, or reduce, these hazards will have taken a large step towards preventing higher frequencies of behaviour disorders.

This chapter will also focus on a number of techniques which the teacher can use effectively to prevent behaviour disorders. Aside from these, it will also be emphasized that many of the strategies presented in this chapter on Mild Behaviour Disorders can also be used in a general fashion in the classroom to help prevent behaviour problems from occurring or escalating. Of particular note are Long and Newman's (1971) strategies for managing surface behaviours and positive reinforcements.

CHAPTER IV

HOW TO DEAL WITH YOUTHS AT RISK

The Child Must Be Trained To Succeed

Human beings tend to form habits quickly. In general, people get used to doing things in a certain way and are unwilling to change their ways of doing things. We develop routine system of accomplishing tasks and we stick to these methods for the rest of our lives. Moreover, we struggle and make numerous mistakes as we learn new tasks or skills.

For example, when learning to ride a bicycle, suppose a parent or a guardian puts training wheel on the child's first bike, the parent or the guardian creates a situation where the child can learn or practice new activity without posing much risk. After several practice in that controlled environment, it is anticipated that the new skills will make a lasting imprint on the child's memory. The new skills can then be performed independently by the child in any given setting. The child's mind and body are now able to perform the task automatically.

That is the author's purpose in this chapter. The skill that is taught to the child is how to succeed academically or in school. The author's is to teach parents and failing students to develop new pattern of behaviour that will enable them to learn successfully or achieve to their fullest God-given potential. Hopefully, this will help youths at high risk from becoming failures at school. Such failures generally lead to feelings of worthlessness, truancy, severe anti-social problems and incarceration. At risk students soon to begin to believe that failure is a normal way of life. They become helpless victims once they become caught in that trap. The purpose of the author in writing this book is to help rescue at risk youths, and to give then opportunity to become academically and socially the kind of successful human beings their families and society want them to be.

The Question Is, How Do We Create Successful Students

As parents, educators or a member of the community, we have to get the youths to act and think in manner that results in academic success. Next, is to create conditions or circumstances that make success way of life for these youths,

In other words, children at risk should be encouraged or lead to develop new behaviour patterns that will lead them to success in school, and in their everyday lives. These at-risk youths should expect success, and they should get success.

Let us make our vulnerable or students-at risk believe that life is worth living, and their beliefs will create the fact. Society expects large numbers of at-risk students not to succeed. Some well-meaning teachers and parents confront the problems of these at-risk students with high resolve and have hopes for those students success Regrettably, it is generally anticipated these students are likely to become school dropouts, and not High School graduates,

The question arises as to how we look at a student who seems to have the signs of continued failure, such as poor grades, bad attitude, and lack of basic skills and expect him or her to be successful?

It would seem that some teachers gain positive control over their own attitudes towards at-risk students. Those teachers, who desire to rescue at-risk students, may need to develop method for building for positive expectations.

This may be achieved through mental imagery, tapes, books, practice and discipline, etc,. Learning with expect guidance may be helpful. The results may worth the effort. For the novice, a very effective method of visualization is achieved through training by an expert. Attempts to rescue students at-risk are pointless as long as failure is expected.

Suggestions for Teachers and Parents with at-risk students

1. The teacher **may let the at-risk youth imagine or create picture success.**

2. **The teacher must now give the at-risk youth a taste of success. The teacher loses if the student succeeds at first. The at-risk student may try once he or she has gotten bogged down to failure. In that case, the teacher should not try talking the child into trying again**

This is primarily due to the fact that failure is a pattern or a habit. At-risk student has learned to think and act in a self-defeating ways. The at-risk child has come to believe that he or she is going to fail despite his/her good efforts. He/she considers himself/ herself as either stupid or lazy or both.

The at-risk student considers his/her situation as utterly hopeless, and can't imagine being successful at school. He/she is convinced that he/she cannot learn. In order to reverse the at-risk student pattern of failure, teachers and parents must try to change the child's way of thinking as well as his/her behaviour. The at-risk student must begin to believe that he or she is perfectly capable of learning. He/ she must acquire a new self-concept that includes the possibilities of success.

Both failure and success are habit forming. In general, students who work very hard are usually successful – they get satisfactory or good grades. The converse is true for the at-risk student who believes that the work is too hard and that he/she is a failure, anyway. Such self-defeating attitude is generally associated students at-risk and those considered to be learning disabled. Just as failure becomes a habit, so is success. In other words, success is auto-reinforcing. Once a student is successful at a task, he/she is motivated to try another task, and expects to be successful. To reverse the failure of the student at-risk, parents and teachers must endeavour to change their thoughts as well as their actions.

Strategies For Rescuing At-risk Students

There are a number of special strategies which a teacher may employ in the classroom to rescue the at-risk students. In combination, these strategies create a charged atmosphere in which the high-risk student is almost bound to be successful.

The first rescue method is, indeed, the beginning step in a process, since it forms the foundation for all other techniques. Its importance cannot be overemphasized. When selecting topics for special projects, when making choices about which skills the teacher should stress, when deciding on materials to introduce a new concept, when the teacher is deciding which aspect of a subject he or she should emphasise, when giving examples, the teacher should choose a topic that is interesting to the student and likely to hold the student's attention.

At-risk students, for the most part, have not tasted academic success are often not motivated. They are trapped in a pattern of failure, and tend to consider schoolwork as stupid and boring. Thus, the at-risk student will not put any effort on tasks he/she considers as stupid and boring. It is clear that the student's attitude ia part of the problem. The at-risk student believes that learning in school has no value for them, and that academic accomplishments are not useful,

These are attitudes of defeat, lack of desire and academic failures. Students at-risk hardly see any correlation between work at school and their personal lives. They don't see how they can gain anything of personal value in the real world by learning in school. In the opinion of the at-risk student, academic accomplishments are not useful. These are attitudes of defeat

The teacher must use strong motivating measures before embarking on any serious programs of instruction, when the at-risk student shows no interest at hand. This is referred to as salesmanship in the world outside the classroom.

Parents and teachers must come to terms with the fact that the at-risk student must have his/her own reasons for wanting to learn something. At times, the teacher deliberately has to provide a picture of the benefits to the student by mastery of the task. Either way, the degree and the amount of progress the student makes is very closely related to how much genuine interest he/she shows in mastering the skill assigned. In particular, the at-risk student must be convinced that an accomplishment is important to his personal life. Otherwise, he is not likely to be interested in mastering the skills. When the at-risk student is convinced that a particular skill is important to his/her personal life, he/she will figure out ways to gain mastery of that task

Challenging the Student

The teacher must ensure that the work he/she assigns to the student offers a real challenge. Teachers often assign tasks to at-risk students that are pointless. The student's motivation has been dealt a severe blow by tasks that serve no purpose other than keeping the students quite and busy. The student's assignment is either so difficult that failure is a certainty or it is so easy that no meaningful learning takes place. At-risk students are seldom given a fair chance for success Such students are not accustomed to real challenges

Students at risk and failing are often described as lazy. To their teachers, parents and the casual observer, it seems as if the at-risk student will do anything to avoid doing schoolwork. In fact, what the at-risk student is trying to avoid is pointless activity.

To love what one does and feel that it matters can be fun and rewarding. In order to break the pattern of failure and feeling of hopelessness, teachers must ensure that all assignments make sense to the at-risk student. Every task must be seen as a step towards a desired goal. The student is likely to do the dullest drill with enthusiasm, if it is perceived as part of the process of a skill that will benefit the student.

Class assignments do not have to be difficult to be challenging. Even small amount of genuine or real effort can make the student succeed. Success can be meaningless, if it is easily attained. When good grades are easily awarded by teachers, students are deprived of the satisfaction of real achievement.

Adjusting teacher's methods and material

The teacher must select methods and materials that likely to be effective, and must be ready to revise those methods and materials, if they do not work. Students at-risk hardly learn successfully with standard classroom methods. Besides, teacher's guides have no suggestions for instructional strategies that work for at-risk students. Also, regular textbooks do not seem compatible with the style of learning of the at-risk student.

The academic failures of these at-risk students clearly support these facts. It would seem, therefore, that a fresh new approach is needed, if the at-risk student is to be rescued. It is the teacher's responsibility to determine the learning style of the at-risk student, then use suitable methods geared to the child's preferences, abilities and interests.

Multi-sensory techniques are believed to be effective with leaching the at-risk students. The chances for success increase tremendously with the at-risk student, by teaching to all the sensory channels. For example, by a touch of colour to writtem material can provide the kind of visual interest that makes the information easier to remember and understand. Instead of underlying the subject once and the verb twice, the teacher can write the nouns in red and the verbs in blue.

Also, when putting mathematical problems on the board, the teacher can make the signs and the process symbols in a bright colour that stands out. The teacher can also encourage the students to take notes in different colours or underline texts with several different highlighters. The introduction of colour makes the material more multi-sensory.

There are students that need to talk their way through thought processing. Teachers should not discourage these students from moving their lips while reading or engaging in discussion with themselves sub-vocally when thinking. It is believed by some experts that verbal cues can help facts stored efficiently in the memory.

Multi-sensory techniques will provide students at-risk a learning boost. However, adjustments in material may be needed also. The teacher must be very sensitive to the feelings of the student about the materials being used. Doing alphabetizing with a phone book or dictionary feels grown-up and important. On the other hand, the same practice with lists in third grade spelling book will be humiliating or degrading to students who are much older. A young student is not likely to succeed, if he/she is forced to use materials he/she dislikes or considers demeaning.

Besides choosing a topic that is certain to attract and holds the students interest, the teacher must select methods and materials that are likely to work. In so doing, the teacher must focus on the idea of "rescue". The reader should bear in mind that a "rescue" is not an attempt to teach something about a particular subject. Rather, the goal is to start a chain reaction with success.

Time Limits Should Be Avoided.

When working with at-risk students, the teacher should avoid time limits. The success of the student should not be dependent on learning something by a particular date. The teacher should allow weeks or months for the student to gain mastery of the materials being used to create the student's first taste if success. The at-risk student has a habit of missing deadlines. However, the teacher's goal in this new approach is competence. It does not matter how long it takes to reach mastery, providing progress is being made.

This is a major departure from the normal approach to instruction in which the pace and the sequence of instruction are controlled by the text. In general, textbooks are written in chapters and units. Textbooks are written in such a way that topics are jumped from one to another. This does not allow the student to stick with one concept until he/she really gets the idea. This may be satisfactory for successful student. However, for those students at-risk, that kind of approach is problematic,

The rate at which the at-risk student learns must be taken into serious consideration, if that child is to succeed. The child must be taught at his/her own speed. This can be achieved by presenting a concept, followed by presentation of the student with materials until he gains complete mastery of the material and he is ready to proceed. This instructional approach is referred to as "conceptual teaching" It has been demonstrated through scientific studies that human brain learns in a conceptual format. It takes in related pieces of information until it catches on to the pattern and recognizes the overall concept. Thus when the student says, "Oh, I now understand it" This results from repetition and practice.

Creating a deadline is not helpful to the student at-risk. Deadlines put pressures and anxiety on the at-risk student. This results in mental shutdown. Failing students tend to develop school-phobia. Undue pressures make the at-risk student nauseated or give such students sweaty palms.

Thus, teachers who place emphasis on competence instead of deadlines create calm atmosphere. This approach eliminates tension and eases anxiety. Freeing the at-risk student from deadlines, pressures and anxiety makes learning a natural process.

What Constitutes Success?

It is absolutely important that the teacher clearly defines success to the students. The student must know what they are asked to learn and what benefit they may gain from the task. There must be no room for disagreement at a later date. The teacher must answer truthfully, if the students want to know if they are making any significant progress, and if the goals of the course are being met. From the very beginning of the course, the teacher must set things up so that success can be recognized.

Teachers must bear in mind that at-risk students perceive themselves as losers. This implies that even when they succeed at a task, they usually shrug it off as mere luck. That is part of the self-defeating attitude that keeps the at-risk student bogged down to constant failures. Such students must not be allowed to think that the academic success they achieve through a rescue is not a fluke. The at-risk student will be able to see his/her own success, if he/she is provided with a clear description the desired goal.

Students with academic failures need something more than academic accomplishments. They need to recognize their own successes and feel that they earned them. They believe that they have the power to achieve success.

Teaching Students At-Risk How To Learn

At-risk students, who generally do not succeed in school do not seem to have developed effective study skills. These students do not have effective learning strategies and techniques that will enable them to learn and succeed. The at-risk students think that their academic failures can be attributed to the fact that they are "dumb' or not bright. They do not realize that they do not know what to do to learn effectively.

Teachers must come to terms with the fact that at-risk students do not learn by standard classroom methods. They must, therefore, be taught study techniques that are bound to result in their academic successes. It is the responsibility of the teacher to teach a method that will enable each student to reach his/her academic goal. In other words, the classroom teacher must be very creative. The teacher may have to experiment with a number of alternative approaches until the effective technique is found. The at-risk student must never be asked to practice until the teacher has shown/him/her how..

Failing students do not know what techniques will enable them to learn and achieve success. Such students are always trapped in their own patterns of failure. They tend to repeat their unsuccessful methods over and over again. Left to their own devices, at-risk students hardly figure techniques that will enable them to learn. The at-risk student will continue to experience failures until the teacher is able to find a way out this academic dead end.

Provision of Good Study Environment

So as to ensure success, a practice routine must be established. The effectiveness of the practice sessions will depend upon on proper control of the environment and the schedule.

In the first place, the teacher must give the student a place where he/she is comfortable, secure and free from any distractions. The student must be encouraged to consider as a special spot for him to reflect, think and study. The teacher must let the student preference determine the location and the type of seating provided as much as possible. Since no two students learn exactly in the same manner, certain factors must always be considered,

Noise

The noise level in the environment is very crucial. For considerable number of students, deep concentration is possible almost anywhere, Such students easily submerged in their work in spite of loudest noises or sounds in their environment. However, only few at-risk students are able to concentrate and work in such an environment, At-risk students are easily distracted.

It is now known that there are some students that actually need noise so as to concentrate. Background sounds from stereo, television, radio, in fact, help these students to study better. There seems to be growing body of evidence that suggests that certain types of music can make all students into better learners..

Light

The amount of light in the student's study room or classroom is of utmost importance. There are students that are unable to concentrate in class unless there is bright and adequate light. Others feel they need real daylight instead of the glow that the light bulbs create. Dim lighting tends to make such students sleepy and sluggish, while bright lighting keeps them alert.

Other students feel that low lighting helps them keep calm and stay focused, while bright light makes them nervous and fidgety. Dim lighting increases concentration of other students.

Temperature

Student's personal preferences regarding room temperature varies, indeed. There are students who fan themselves and complain of excessive heat, while others shiver. Thus, the room temperature must be adequately adjusted to make the students comfortable.

Seating

Standard formal classroom seating is not suitable for all students/ It may be convenient for the teacher to have the whole class seated in chairs. However, it may be helpful to encourage at-risk students to explore alternative postures.

Oral Stimulation

Some people are of the opinion that we think much better, when our thinking process is accompanied by the mouth. For example, when concentrating, some people may chew a gum or bite their fingers. It is believed by some that such activities have positive influence on the nervous system. Food and beverages are not normally available in the classroom, however, some believe that some at-risk students may benefit from such an intake,

Teacher Managed Intervention

It is important for classroom teachers and other school personnel who are concerned about the needs of individual students who deviate significantly in some way from what is expected in their assigned grade for their chronological age to recognize that in each area of development, cognitive, affective, and psychomotor, there is a wide range of normal behaviour. Some students' behaviour can deviate from teachers and parents expectation and yet not present a special problem.

The term at-risk of school failure refer to those students, who without special attention, are likely to have increasing difficulty in school to the point where they will fail academically, and have severe problems associated with socialization and self esteem. Eventually they do not complete the education which is appropriate for their competence level.

This chapter addresses issues that are related to home and school environment, health, learning and temperament. Students who are at risk present a diverse picture; the issues or solutions are not simple. However, by recognizing that intervention must follow assessment, and that once the student problems become clear they will be more manageable. The intervention should fit into a natural process that most teachers can implement, particularly when other sources of support are available in the school.

In the event the problems are complex or require more time and knowledge than the classroom teacher has at his or her disposal, the teacher should be prepared to know precisely what type of help is needed, and in what area to make referral for assistance.

The Decision Making Process

The teacher must try to identify:

1. which students in the classroom might be at risk of school failure
2. specific problems of concern
3. help the student to determine:
4. which type of intervention framework will be most effective
5. specific tactics for intervention

Always consider the classroom environment as well as physical and sensory disorders to ascertain factors which might influence the student's behaviour. Other areas of concern which the teacher must consider include:

1. family and welfare issues
2. school and classroom environment
3. physical and sensory disorders
4. developmental and learning disorders
5. temperament and behaviour disorders

Moving from assessment to intervention, the teacher must highlight areas of concern in three areas:

1. divide concerns into three areas
2. checklist titles under each area indicating specific contents
3. checklist titles under each area indicating specific contents
4. behavioural checklist index listing problem behaviour/ presenting signs which direct the teacher to various checklists containing those behaviours
5. checklists which most completely address the individual student's constellation of behaviours are then used.

Family and Welfare Issues

The cause of the student's problem may not be related to the school or academic program. More hours are spent out of the classroom than in, and for some students they can be difficult. Consider whether these or similar factors are a concern with your student.

1. New to the community and not adjusting well
2. Recent loss of good friends or family member
3. Recent traumatic experiences
4. Problems at home or in their neighbourhood
5. Turmoil due to family quarrels, family worries, difficulty with jobs
6. Poor health
7. Disagreement with siblings or parents
8. Physical violence, neglect, or sexual abuse.

Classroom Environment Factors

The teacher should consider whether the physical attributes of the school and the classroom, including the stressors in his or her own life, are conducive to the student's learning. Some of the following should be considered:

Classroom temperature
Classroom acoustics
Comfort of classroom furniture
Factors influencing allergic conditions

Physical/Sensory Disorders

This area includes health problems, physical disorders and sensory disorders. Any problems that interfere with the student being in good physical condition will interfere with stamina, coordination and ability to perform and interest in schoolwork. The teacher should take into account:

Illness
Poor medical care
Hearing problems
Vision problems
Movement problems
Poor nutrition.

Developmental and Learning Disorders

Developmental disorder can arise in the areas of affect, cognition, language and psychomotor skills. Often, early and intense intervention can alleviate many problems, but without help children may evidence increasingly severe problems. Some of the possibilities to consider are:

Students' emotional maturity
Delays in development of language and psychomotor skills
Students who cannot handle demands of group instruction
Students who may not deal effectively with large group of peers
The complete variety of specific learning problems.

Temperament and Behaviour Disorders

Students who often cause the most difficulty are those who are noncompliant and create management problems. Difficulties in these areas usually have their roots somewhere else; if the history of the student could be examined it might show a problem at home, a physical sensory disorder, or an attention or learning disorder. Issues of self-esteem are very important. It would be a mistake to ignore underlying factors when a student has a temperament disorder. Such students may need altered expectations, task demands and pressure or environment where there is more appropriate stimulation.

The teacher must consider all the possibilities that could create the following:

Physical, developmental, learning and temperament delays and deviances, hyperactivity, inattention, impulsivity, irritability, and poor habit regulation can cause difficulties for the child.

While acting out students have always been the focus of attention because of the sometimes immediate need to address their behaviour, there are many other ways in which students indicate they have problems;

Fearfulness and anxiety

Depression
Lack of concentration
Lack of impulse control
Poor self control in the form of stealing, or gambling or other antisocial behaviours
Substance abuse.

Although the areas of risk are divided into five categories, the intent of the teacher should not to diagnose and label his/her students but to focus on sets of behaviour that can serve as basis for assessment, planning and intervention, and program evaluation. There will be some areas where students suspected difficulties must be referred to an expert as soon as possible. They include child abuse, sensory disorders and medical issues.

REFERENCES

At-Risk Group, A Successful pathway For All Students. Toronto: Ontario Ministry of Education, 2003.

Beauchemin, Claire. Give them A Reason to Stay. Ajax, Ontario: Educational Research Council, 1989.

Benedict, Richard. Trashcan Kids. Alexandria, VA: Association for Supervision and Curriculum, 1992

Bleuer, Jeanne C, Schreiber, Penny, et al. Young Students At-Risk. Ann Arbor, MI: ERIC Clearinghouse, 1989.

Brendiro, Larry et al. Reclaiming Youth At-Risk: Our Hope For the Future. Bloomington, IN: National Education Service, 1990

Brown, Roberts. Mentoring At Risk Students: Challenges and Potential. Toronto: Toronto Board of Education, 1995.

Chall, Jeanne, et al. Reading Crisis: Why Poor Children Fall Behind. Cambridge, Mass. Harvard University Press, 1990.

Dornai, Angie, et al. Students At Risk Effective Strategies and Programs. Toronto: OSST, 2001.

Kozol, Jonathan, Savage Inequalities: Children in American School. New York: Harper Perennial, 1992

Kuykendall, Crystall. From Rage to Hope: Strategies for Reclaiming Black and Hispanic Students. Bloomington, IN: National Educational Services, 1992.

BEHAVIOUR/EMOTIONAL DISORDERS

Definition of Behaviour/Emotional Disorders

A definition of behaviour disorders may suggest two main factors. The first is an understanding or a perspective on why humans behave the way they do, and the reason for providing the definition, As an educator, and a trained educational psychologist, the behaviour which occurs in the classroom is of primary interest to the writer, although arguably the same general principles, would hold in other environments. Regarding an educational perspective on the definition emphasis will be on those situations that results from the students' interaction with the educational environment and process, the effects of which limits the benefits the students derive their educational experience.

There are many and complex factors that contribute to a behaviour disorder. These range from the characteristic of the people involved, to the characteristics of the educational environment. Students are likely to act and react in unique ways in different situations, since they are unique individuals. Also, teachers, school counsellors, parents, school administrators and resource personnel, are unique individuals, and also likely to act and react differently depending on the circumstances. Thus, the characteristics of all these unique individuals will play a significant role in a behaviour disorder, since these individuals interact with each other in the context of the educational process.

One should not overlook the characteristics of the environment, such as rules, routines, physical structure, and performance expectations in any behaviour. Thus, behaviour disorder as viewed by the writer is defined in a practical manner and expressed in terms of the number of situational characteristics, which when present in sufficient degree, disrupts or have negative impact on the educational process.

By defining behaviour disorder this way, a functional definition is presented, which also, reflects the purpose. This suggests that

behaviour disorder is defined in a practical manner so as to enable the classroom teacher to arrive at best possible informed decisions concerning. Identification, assessment and correction of the disordered behaviour or situation.

Moreover, behaviour disorders are defined along a continuum since teachers face many problems in their classroom which may not, on the surface appear severely disruptive but which, if ignored could escalate to point where they may be very costly to the teacher and the student. The advantages of such a definition are based on the assumption that, being functional and broadly based, the definition corresponds directly to the situation at hand. This implies that the teacher and others who may be associated not only define behaviour disorders based on their experiences, but also construct a functional framework for making informed decision in regards to identification, assessment and correction at the same time.

In the schools, a behaviour disorder takes place when students respond to the educational environment in ways that significantly deviates from age-appropriate expectations, and which interfere with their own learning as well as others. Behaviour disorder is viewed along a continuum since all students exhibit, demonstrate inappropriate behaviour at some time in some places

One end of the continuum represents situations within which students exhibit such behaviours infrequently and briefly, in relatively few settings to a mild degree. The other end of the continuum represents a much smaller of situations within which students exhibit such behaviour with high frequency, for extended period of time, in many situations, and to an extreme degree.

The teacher may conclude that as the level of the severity of the behaviour disorder increases, so should the extent and the nature of the intervention or corrective strategy. Mild behaviour disorders may best be corrected in the regular classroom setting, with support to the family and the teacher as may be necessary. Other measures may be required as the level of the severity of the behaviour disorder increases. Such measures include resource personnel, behavioural aides, clinical and residential classes, as well as special classes. The required interventions in situations of mild behaviour disorder may be informal and brief. However, in situations of severe behaviour disorder, intervention can be expected to be both intensive and prolonged,

The severity of a behaviour disorder is judged in terms of its effects on the education of the student rather than being based strictly on the characteristics of the particular behaviour. Due to the many subjectivity factors in the definition and the identification, a precise standard definition of the "Mild," "Moderate," and "Severe" is not possible. However, what is possible is the provision of examples of each of each degree or level to assist teachers in making their own decision. The severity of a behaviour disorder may be considered in terms of characteristics, which either individually or in various combinations, typically characterize behaviour disorders.

These characteristics are:

the demonstration of inability to establish or maintain satisfactory relationships with peers or adults;

the demonstration of general mood of unhappiness or depression;

the demonstration of inappropriate behaviour or feelings under ordinary conditions;

the demonstration of a continued difficulty in coping with the learning situation in spite of remedial intervention;

the demonstration of physical symptoms or fear associated with personal or school issues;

the demonstration of difficulties in accepting the realities of personal responsibilities and accountability.

In the preceding, the writer has discussed behaviour disorder from a generalized perspective. To facilitate the process of identification, assessment and correction of behaviour disorders, it is essential to complement this generalized perspective with description of any behaviour. Ii must be emphasized that all behaviour whether positive or problematic, can be analyzed in terms of seven observable dimensions which include 1context, 2.complexity, 3.directionality, 4.intensity, 5. frequency, 6. duration, 7. consistency.

The key to identifying, assessing and correcting a behaviour disorder is the analysis of the behaviour disorder in terms of the seven dimensions previously discussed. A description of these seven dimensions are as follows:

Context. Context may be viewed as the relationship of the behaviour disorder to the ongoing process of environmental events. Context may be specifically defined in terms of the behaviour events which provide and follow specified behaviours which constitute the behaviour disorder. This implies that context identifies and defines the antecedents of the behaviour which is producing the disruption, and the consequences of the behaviour in the environment.

Complexity: This refers to the variety of the specific behaviours which are observed to be part of the behaviour disorder. Some behaviour disorders are simple in that there is but a single specific behaviour which requires correction. The corrective program, therefore, would be developed to reduce or eliminate the behaviour. The fact that there is one behaviour only does not necessarily imply the behaviour disorder would be defined as mild.

Depending on its other dimensions, a single behaviour such as poking with a sharp object could be defined as severe. Behaviour disorders become more difficult to deal with as complexity increases.

The various components of the behaviour disorder would have to be priorized in terms of developing an overall corrective strategy.

Directionality: The directionality of the behaviour refers to those individuals affected by the behaviour. Individuals affected may be a student, the teacher and other students. A situation can be collectively be more severe. For example, the escalation of disruptive behaviour can lead to a tense classroom atmosphere where once harmony and peacefulness existed.

Corrective strategies will vary as the directionality of the behaviour disorder varies. Where other students are affected and involved, they may have to be taught how to respond to the inappropriate behaviour as part of the corrective strategy. Likewise, as the behaviour disorder involves the interaction between the student and teacher, changes in the teacher's behaviour will have to be given serious consideration.

Intensity: Intensity may be defined in terms of how disturpting a particular behaviour is. While intensity is in part a quantitative dimension of behaviour, e.g. how loudly a student argues with the teacher, it is also to a large degree qualitative and subjective. For example, it will be difficult to measure how loudly a student argues. In lieu of a quantitative measure of intensity, it is possible to qualitatively distinguish between arguing in a normal, raised, or screaming voice. Similarly, a student's poking behaviour may be characterized or defined as aggravating, annoying or hurtful.

Thus, the definition of intensity is particularly susceptible to the subjective perception of the teacher. If the teacher is having a particular good day, behaviour disorders are more likely to be viewed as less intense due to the teacher's greater degree of tolerance. The same behaviour at a different time, or in a different classroom with a different teacher may be viewed as more as more intense or disturbing. Some teachers structure the classroom so that so that students are encouraged to argue rationally, and even a raised voice is often reinforced for its demonstration of student commitment to a point of view. Other teachers structure their classrooms with much stricter rules about the questioning of rules, regulations and authority. While most students can adjust to the varying demands and expectations of different teachers at different time, students who are vulnerable to behavioural disorders experience have considerable difficulty when expectations vary and change without clear explanation. Intensity as well as other dimensions of a behaviour disorder, therefore, is much a product of teacher s as it is of student characteristics.

Consistency: Consistency refers to how to how typical the behaviour disorder is in totality of the student's experience, particularly in terms of the number and types of different environments in which the behaviour occurs. A functional definition will indicate whether the behaviour disorder occurs in one particular classroom, in all classrooms, on the school grounds, in the community at large and/ or in the home. The strategies for assessment and correction will vary as a function of the consistency of the behaviour disorder simply because more people will have to be involved. A general rule is that the more consistent or pervasive a behaviour disorder is, the more structured assessment and correction will have to be.

Frequency: Frequency is simply how often a specific behaviour occurs, and if the behaviour is operationally defined, ie. defined in terms of which allow for direct measurement, frequency can be measured as easily by a variety of methods. In the identification of a behaviour disorder, however, statements about frequency can be misleading, particularly if they are not operationally defined.

Duration is a measure of how long each episode of the behaviour may last. Duration may be short. Poking someone, for example, may last only one second per episode because it may be a single jab in the leg of a student sitting next to the offender. On the other hand, the duration per episode may be longer, as in the case where poking is defined as a series of multiple jabs in rapid succession until the other student cries out in pain or annoyance. In each instance, the selection of a corrective strategy may be different. Another example of duration may be considered in a situation where a teacher identifies the problem subjectively.

Identification, Assessment, and Program Planning for the Behaviourally Disordred Child.

The earlier discussion of behaviour was aimed at providing a framework for the functional identification of behaviour disorders. The identification process itself involves two steps. First, the teacher needs a strategy for the initial clarification and definition of a situation which he or she has become aware of and is concerned about it. Consideration of the seven dimension of behaviour disorder will facilitate the teacher's definition of the situation in terms of its potential for formal assessment and intervention.

It may occur that, during this first step, the teacher recognizes the potential for escalation and, and without formal procedures, is able to take preventive or corrective action. It may also be the case that that this first step will result in a "red flag", a caution for the teacher to be alert for repeated episode and escalation.. While conducting an identification process, it should be noted that one negative episode does not constitute a behaviour disorder..

The next step in the identification process requires the teacher to make a decision whether or not to proceed with a formal assessment, the fact remains that a formal assessment is time consuming, and that resources to conduct an assessment are often in high demand and in short supply.

To assist the teacher conduct an identification process, including using his or her judgement as to whether a formal assessment is called for, an identification checklist may be helpful

Assessment:, The process of assessment, program planning and evaluation are closely related and, for this reason, are considered jointly in this section. Assessment may be defined as the process of gathering information and stating what the problem is;. Program planning, on the other hand, is specifying how the problem can be corrected; while evaluation is the process of determining the effect, or impact, of the corrective strategy. The eventual program plan depends on the methods used to assess. In view of these interdependencies, the process of assessment is critical.

As in the process of identification, assessment involves both objective data as well as subjective perceptions and impressions. Also, assessment is based on an analysis of the seven dimensions of behaviour discussed earlier. The primary difference between assessment and identification is that assessment is more formalized, structured and systematic.

The purpose of an assessment is to gain specific information about the student and his or her situation in order to facilitate informed decision making by those sharing responsibility for corrective measures. The assessment process will vary as the relative severity of the relative severity of the behaviour disorder varies. For mild behaviour disorders, assessment may be relatively informal and limited in scope, based on those obvious dimensions of which the teacher readily identifies as the key to the problem.

In these instances, the need for documentation may be minimal since these instances are those which occur infrequently in any classroom. On the other hand, if behaviour disorders are more severe, the process of assessment will be more formal and extensive and will require documentation. The point is that informed decision-making is often a matter of good common sense with mild behaviour disorders, but usually a rigorous and challenging task in severe cases.

One objective of an assessment is to enable the development of a functional plan for correction which would: 1), identify the specifics of the behaviour disorder in terms of the dimensions of behaviour; 2), efficiently communicate the information about the behaviour disorder in terms of the seven dimensions of behaviour and, 3).specify the corrective strategy.

A second objective of the assessment is to provide a framework for the evaluation of the corrective strategy. This implies that method used to assess the behaviour disorder would also be used to determine the effect of the corrective strategy.

Consistent with the definition of behaviour disorder previously discussed, a functional framework for the assessment of behaviour disorders is based on the rational that:

1.behaviour disorders exist within the interaction between the student and his or her educational environment, and are the result of conflict between the student and his or her educational environment. Conflict is defined as the product of opposing sets of behavioural standards and/or expectations;

2. corrective strategies will focus on the student as well as the student's environment, which may include classroom, the school, the community at large, and/or the home; and

3.correction of the behaviour disorder will be achieved by changing aspects of the environment or, in most instances, changing both to a certain degree. Environment is defined as all the persons, objects and events existing together in time and space.

REFERENCES

Axelrod, Behaviour Identification for the Classroom Teacher, New York: McGraw-Hill, 1977

Bernstein, G.S, et al. Behaviour Habilitation Through Proactive Programming. Baltimore, Md.:Brookes, 1981.

Bernstein, G.S.et al. Behavioural Rehabilitation Through Proactive Programming. Baltimore, Md: Brookes, 1981.

Cartwright, C.A., and Cartwright, G.P. Developing Observation Skills. New York: McGraw-Hill, 1974.

Clarizio, H.F and McCoy, G..M. Behaviour Disorders in Chiildren (2nd edi.).Nwe York: Crowell, 1976.

Csapo, M. Children With Behaviour and Social Disorders. A Canadian Focus, Vancouver, B.C, Center For Human Development and Research, 1981.

Cutela, J.R. Behaviour Analysis Forms for Clinical Intervention. Champaign, Ill.: Research Press. 1977.

Dreikurs, R. Psychology in the Classroom: A Manual for Teacher (2nd. ed.). New York: Harper and Row, 1968.

Ellis, A, Wolfe, J.L, and Mosley, S. How to raise an emotionally,,Healthy, Happy Child. Hollywood, C.A.:Wilshire, 1974.

Flanders,, N. Analyzing Teacher Behaviour. Menlo Park. Calif.: Addison-Wesley, 1970.

Hanmill, D.D; Bartel, N.R and Bunch, G.O. Teaching Children with Learning and Behaviour Problems. (Canadian Edition), Toronto. Ont.: Allyn and Bacon, 1984.

Kendall, P.C.and Norton-Ford, J.D.: Clinical Psychology: Scientific and Professional Dimensions. New York: John-Wiley, 1982.

Kessler, J.W. Psychopathology of Childhood. Englewood Cliffs. N.J: Prentice-Hall, 1966.

Losen, M.., and Diament, B. Parent Conferences in Schools. Boston: Allyn and Bacon, 1978.

McCallon, E., and McGray, E. Planning and Conducting Interviews. Austin, Texas: Learning Concepts, 1975.

Newcomer, P.L Understanding and Teaching Emotionally Disturbed Children. Boston, Mass.: Allyn Bacon, 1980.

One Giant Step: The Integration of Children with Special Needs. Program 10: The Behaviourally Disordered, Alberta Education, 1983

Simonson, L.R. A Curriculum Model for Individuals with Severe Learning and Behaviour Disorders. Baltimore, Md.: University Park Press, 1979.

Stephens, L.R. Hartman, A.C.and Lucas, V.H. Teaching Basic Skills: A Curriculum Handbook. Columbus, Ohio Charles E. Merrill, 1978.

CHAPTER V

SPECIAL EDUCATION SERVICES

In most cases, high-risk students are placed in special education programs in school. What then is Special Education or what are the goals of special education?

Special Education refers to education of children with special needs children who may be gifted or talented or students who are handicapped or who may have academic challenges. It is intended for a relatively a small number of the student population. Special education may differ from general education in a couple of significant ways.

In order to understand the nature and scope of Special Education, it may be helpful if we consider the background of general education against which special education is set. In most school jurisdictions, the education of most children has traditionally been provided through group instruction in classes in locally operated schools. These schools make use of state or provincially developed or approve curricula.

The goals and the objectives which are considered for the students serve to guide the development of curricula. It is anticipated that these curricula in the hands of well trained and competent teachers, will be able to meet the educational needs and interests of a wide variety of students. Special education is aimed at serving that relatively small proportion of students whose needs cannot be met adequately by the regular classroom program. High-risk students and exceptional students may need special curricula and instructional methodology

Is sensitive to the effects of physical conditions in the room, and how that may affect the learning of the student.

Able to minimize the student dependence on the teacher that ia appropriate to the level of handicap.

Assessment, Objectives and Program Planning

Ascertain student's strengths' strengths and weaknesses in at least five areas,

Information obtained from standard testing instruments may be used to assist with instructional planning.

The assessment data may be used to profile the students' strengths and weaknesses in setting up individualized educational programs.

The teacher's interactions must be recorded and interpreted.

The learning tasks must be analysed and should be broken down into smaller components; and the specific instructional objectives should be written down for each student.

The teacher must demonstrate initiative and resourcefulness in planning the students' curriculum, which must be based on reasonable short-term and long-term goals.

Teaching and the Learning Situations

Can teach the attending behaviour with one student, and in group setting.

Able to teach a lesson that includes all of the essential steps.

He/she uses the appropriate positive feedback, which is immediate and task relevant.

Can use modeling and cuing strategies, and can shape new behaviours.

Able to use punishment and extinction procedures appropriately for modifying/decreasing behaviour

Can individualize instruction within a group structure.

Able to select relevant teaching materials, and can use instructional media appropriately.

Evaluation and Records.

Demonstrate an initiation in keeping out opportunities for improving teaching skills.

Daily lessons and activities involving aides in operational changes must be evaluated.

Ability to evaluate program effectiveness in terms of the student's learning and behaviour.

Keeping record of the child's performance using criterion-referenced and standardized data.

Involvement of Parents.

One must demonstrate sensitivity as to how parents feel about their children's disability.

Make adequate and sufficient preparation for meeting with parents.

Prepare parents for classroom visits, and follow up on parent meetings.

Report students progress to parents in a positive but **objective** manner.

Alternative Placement for Students with Special Educational Needs

There are educators who have stressed the importance of integrating students with special education needs with regular academic students as much as possible. This is generally referred to as 'mainstreaming'. A considerable number of parents, educators and students are of the view that the previous reliance of using self-contained or segregated programs to serve students with special educational needs is retrogressive and undesirable.

This suggests the need to integrate or mainstream students with special educational needs as well as gifted and talented into the regular school program. However, those students who may have special educational needs, such as more support or protection, than can be provided in the regular classroom program, a series of fully or semi-segregated classroom options had been suggested.

One of the objectives of special education assessment is to ascertain what placement will best serve the student who has special needs. The most important of the special education instructional program is to assist the student with special educational needs as much as possible It is also aimed at moving the student toward less protective settings with the ultimate goal of obtaining placement in the regular classroom. It must, at the same time be recognized that settings with more specialized assistance may be more appropriate for some students

The support that may be required for a special needs student who may be mainstreamed in the regular classroom may vary according the student's needs. It may include special teaching techniques. The special needs student who is mainstreamed may be in jeopardy when requirement for extra support are not provided.

REFERENCES

Alberta Association for Children and Adults with Learning Disabilities. Partners in Education. Principles for a New School Act, June 1985.

Alberta Education. School Grants Regulations, 1986

Alberta Education.Special Education Handbook.1982

Alberta Education.Special Education Manual, 1987

Anything Can Be: The Idea of Identification and Remediation of Learning Disabilities in the Classroom. Ottawa, Canada Canadian Association for Learning Disabilities: Bell Canada, 1980.

Cruickshank, William, ed. Psychology of Exceptional Children and Youth.3rd Ed. Englewood, Cliffs. NJ; Prentice Hall, 1971.

Csapo, Marg.; Gogech, L ed. Special Education Across Canada.; Issues and Concerns for the 1980s. Vancouver: Center for Human Development and Research, 1980.

Day, Catherine, et al. Educating Exceptional Children. Scarborough: Nelson Canada, 1985.

Davis, William, E. The Special Education Strategies for Succeeding in Today's Schools. Austin: Pro Ed, 1983.

Davidson, Ian, et al. Learning Disabilities Identification and Intervention. Toronto: Ministry of Education, 1981.

Duke, D. L. 'What is the nature of educational excellence and should we try it?' Phi Delta Kappan, June 1985, 671-674.

Federation of Women Teachers Association of Ontario.. Position on Special Education. Toronto. 1983.

Hambleton, Doris; Hickson, Mary. Total Commission with Trainable Retarded Children. Toronto: Research Dept., Metropolitan School Board, 1978.

Harvey, Louis, Children and Youth with Special Needs: Summary Report of Findings. Ottawa:Canadian Council on Social Development, 2007.

Hehir, Thomas; Latus. Thomsa, eds. Special Education at the Century's End: Evolution of Theory and Practice since 1970. Cambridge, MA: Harvard Educational Review, 1992

Johnson,D.J and Myklebust, H.R, Learning Disabilities:Educational Principles and Practices. New York Grune & Stratton, 1967

MacKay, A.W.Education Laws in Canada. Emond Montgomery Publishing, 1984,

MbBride, S.R. Evaluating Special Education: Love is not enough, Canadian School Executive, March, 1986,13-15.

Turner, D.G. Legal Issues in the education of the Handicapped. Bloomington, Indiana: Phi Delta Kappa Foundation, 1983

CHAPTER VI

LEARNING AND DEVELOPMENTAL DISORDERS

This chapter will address six areas that are related to developmental and learning disabilities which cover a wide a wide spectrum of abilities.

It also addresses specific learning disabilities, attention deficits, and hyperactivity separately for purpose of assessment of assessment and intervention, although in reality they are often seen simultaneously. A student who has poor attending skills is going to have problems learning, which does not mean a true learning disability is present. A student with a specific learning disability may be able to attend but has great difficulty interpreting as a result, additional behaviour problems may ensue. It is important to address the root of the learning deficit by incorporating a variety of strategies to assist the learning disabled student.

Indicators of Learning Difficulties

The following suggest possible learning problems:

Student has average or better intelligence

Discrepancy of at least one year between achievement and intellectual ability in one or more areas

Uneveness in academic performance: good in arithmetic/poor in reading; speaks well/difficulty with handwriting.

Specific errors in reading and writing such as omissions and substitutions of sounds, reversing letters or sounds; reading words from right to left may suggest learning difficulty.

He/she is uncoordinated; may appear clumsy and may have:

Memory problems; may not remember instructions or be able to repeat sound or picture sequences.

Disorganized in thinking, written work, and actions.

Diffiiculties in reading comprehension.

Unable to focus for appropriate periods of time.

Perseverates on one topic or part of a task.

Difficulty studying on own.

Lack of confidence in own abilities

Overcompensates (i.e., memorizes pages and pretends to read).

Emotional lability (rapid mood changes).

Criteria for action

The teacher should observe the student over a period of time and determine whether he or she has several of the behaviours indicated previously. It should be noted that of one, or even a few of the items may not imply that the student has a problem in that area. It is a combination of factors occurring together over a period of time and to an extreme degree that should be cause for action. In the area of student anxiety, the teacher should implement some of the suggestions provided earlier and see if they can make a difference. If the student begins to feel more comfortable in school the problem may take care of itself. If not, action beyond the classroom should be discussed with school administration.

Specific learning disability is a disorder that involves one or more of the basic psychological processes to understand or use spoken or written language. The disorder may manifest itself in an imperfect ability to listen, think, read, write, speak, spell or do mathematical calculations. The term includes such conditions as perceptual handicaps, brain injury, minimal brain dysfunction, developmental reading, writing and arithmetic disorders and developmental aphasia.

Students with learning disability may have problems specifically related to learning skills such as perception, co-ordination, memory, reasoning, organization and planning. They may also experience difficulties in attention and/or concentration.

Advice for the teacher and other specialists working with the student falls into three main categories:

Interpersonal.
Learning skills.
Classroom management.

Interpersonal – how the student is treated as a person.

Focus on students as individuals. Group comparisons may increase negative self-esteem or negative feelings about personal, social and academic accomplishments. Because students with learning disabilities fail so often it is easy to fall into the quicksand of poor self-image. They learn to be helpless, or give up responsibility for learning. They do not expect to achieve.

Classroom Management – how the teacher manages the total classroom setting so the student can be an integral part of the group without having negative experiences as result of academic problems.

Add additional technical and personnel resources. These may include the use of a computer and resource periods.

Have a place such as a carrel, for the student to work without distractions. This can be as simple as a desk placed in the corner of the room with a corrugated board around the sides to keep out sight and sound distractions. If the student has an urge to diverge they should feel free to go to the carrel and work.

Peer tutoring and peer support can be helpful if the student is willing to accept such assistance and if the provider is given some good assistance techniques.

Do not aggravate the situation. The teacher should try not to antagonize the student. The teacher should determine whether his or her behaviour adds to the problem. For example, the teacher should not single out students when the teacher knows the student cannot answer a particular problem and perform well..

The teacher must encourage the students to perform tasks which the can be successful such as doing errands in the school..

Discuss rules for their classroom behaviour:

How to treat others.

Be positive
Respect others

Learning Skills – The teacher can help the student succeed by teaching him or her to approach tasks in modified ways. Remediation must work in conjunction with classroom management techniques.

In determining a plan for remediation, the teacher should consult with others, such parents, other teachers who know and understand the student. The teacher must be realistic; and should not give assignment to students that he or she knows the students cannot complete without help or for which they do not have the resources.

Students need to take responsibility for their own learning. They must be active participants and feel part of the process. One way to do this is to draw up a contract for completing assignments, doing homework, or working on other classroom behaviours. The teacher and the student agree on terms and both sign.

Specify objectives:

1. Who
2. Will do what
3. To what extent
4. Under what circumstances?

Identify the specific area that is deficient. The teacher should note persistent error patterns in written or spoken work, e.g., word retrieval, sequencing, oral reports. Has the students' problem with sounds (articulations) or ideas (conceptual)?

The teacher must analyze the task; and break it down to small sequential steps in which the student can show success. The teacher must teach the student self-monitoring skills in the areas of deficit.

What is my problem area
What specific errors am I making
The teacher may allow the student to tape and play back to monitor as a self-monitoring device.
That should be done privately.

The teacher should prepare individual drills for practice on a level at which the student practice correct responses. Students should feel free to ask questions or ask for demonstrations when they do not understand. When students are able to perform a skill with 85 to 90 percent accuracy, they can then be encouraged to practice independently with periodic supervision.

If the student tends to be concrete, the teacher must demonstrate what he or she meant by pictures or actions followed by concrete learning strategies. If the student has spatial problems, he or she must be given activities to get involved physically, e.g., music and touch activities.

The teacher can modify the curriculum so that the student succeds. The teacher must work on orderly process of thought and expression. The teacher should allow students to keep record of their gains. In the beginning, some students may need tangible reinforcement to help sustain minimal gains.

Assistance for the family is important if family members are able to help. Parents, siblings and other family members may need to be taught strategies and how to structure their time with the student. If this is going to be stressful for either the student or family it might be best to work out other ways for involvement. Family members can provide materials, help in the classroom, employ a tutor or arrange special learning experiences.

The teacher must first notify school administrator first, when a problem is identified and further assistance is needed. Following advice of the administration, decisions may be made as to how the teacher should proceed.

ATTENTION DEFICIT DISORDERS.

This disorder has been briefly discussed earlier when discussing the work of the psychologist following referral that may include diagnosis of attention deficit disorder. However, in view of the prevalence in the schools and concerns of teachers and parents as well as learning challenges that this disorder creates, it will further discussed here.

Indicators of Attention Deficit Disorders

Appears detached from class activities

Thoughts wander

Difficult to direct to task

Inattentive.

Disregards directions

Problems becoming involved in task

Not goal oriented

Easily distracted

Attention span inappropriate for age.

Approaches task in idiosyncratic ways

Perseverates

Preoccupied with insignificant details

Distracting behaviours

Has unique learning styles.

Criteria for Action

The teacher should observe the student over a period of time and determine whether he or she has several of the behaviours listed earlier. A display of one, or even few, of the items may not imply that the student has a problem in this area. It is a combination of factors occurring together, over a period of time and to an extreme degree that should be cause for action. When the student's needs are addressed his or her attention problems may improve. If not, action beyond the classroom should be discussed with the school administration.

Possible Reasons for the student's behaviour
There are a variety of areas to explore when a student shows indications of an attention deficit disorder. An immediate concern is the possibility of a hearing or vision problem. Other physical problems can also interfere with the student's ability to concentrate.

Another possibility is that of a learning problem. Frequently a learning problem goes in tandem with a problem in attention. Thus, the first step for the teacher is to identify the specific area that is problematic. In addition to paying attention to the indicators mentioned earlier, the teacher can make notes of his or her own observations. For example, the student may have:

Selective attention – In this case, the student is unable to select relevant stimulus dimensions from the irrelevant and maintain attention to these dimensions. Some students may attend to a single stimulus while excluding all relevant stimuli; others may attend to too many aspects. Both over inclusive and over exclusive attention are problems.

Short attention spans – the student may be unable to concentrate on any one task beyond the point where it is appropriate. The student may repeat whatever he/she has done over and over. In the beginning the student is going to need a lot of external monitoring as well as exposure to methods that will improve his or her own self-monitoring. The student will need materials that are programmed and in an interesting way and will allow him or her to move on to the next step. The student may need an environment that is less stimulating.

Self-control Skills:
If the student is going to improve, he/she needs to learn skills related to focusing and concentration. These skills are also applicable to hyperactive and disruptive behaviours. These skills or exercises do

not directly improve the student's ability to do academic work such as math and reading. However, they will allow the teacher to have better instructional control, thus promoting a better atmosphere for learning. Some of the strategies used are role playing, games, and discussion.

Perceive incoming information correctly
Follow instructions
State differences in shapes
Identify likenesses in abstract pictures
Complete pictures

Memory exercises
Hide the bean game
Identification imbedded objects
Flashcards picture recall
Repeating musical sounds

Time orientation, visual, and auditory sequencing.
Calendar work
Picture Sequencing

Anticipating consequences
Discuss the choice of responses
Complete stories
Work on mazes

Relaxing
Physical relaxation exercises
Music stories.

Suggestions for intervention

The teacher may consider the following:

Start or below the level at which the student is performing.

Increase difficulty gradually, use small steps

Present tasks in developmental sequence

Provide positive feedback or praise when appropriate

Recognize efforts as well as successes

Begin each task with a brief review

Assure that task is meaningful and interesting

Be flexible; do not allowed the student to become bored and restless

Have short, frequent, regular training

Consider transfer of training.

Sources of Support

School Administration : The teacher should notify the school administrator when a problem is identified and further assistance is needed. Following advice of administration, decisions may be made as to how the teacher should proceed.

Any of the following may be useful.

Subject area specialists:
Reading teacher
Speech-language pathologist
Learning disabilities specialists

Family members: Family members should be able to provide a history of the problem and the current treatment or outside services the student is receiving. It is necessary to rule out physical illness, and sensory deficit by a duly qualified physician..

ATTENTION DEFICIT DISORDER WITH HYPERACTIVITY.

Indicators of Attention Deficit Disorder with Hyperactivity

Extreme overactivity, and always on the go.

Very fidgety and restless

Does not stay seated, and may wander around the room.

Talks a lot. He/she speaks out impulsively

Does not stay on task for an appropriate period of time

He or she is easily diverted from work; and he rarely finishes task. Also, he or she does not attend to full directions for task completion,

He/she is poorly organized and messy. He/she loses things needed for work

He/she disrupts other students at play.

He or she has hard time waiting foe turn.

He/she does not consider the consequences of dangerous activities

He or she has poor eye-hand coordination

Such students generally do poorly in schoolwork.

He or she works better in one-on-one teaching situation.

Criteria to take action

The teacher should notice within a short period whether the student has several of the hyperactive behaviours listed earlier. However, it should be remembered that a display of one, or even a few, of the items may not mean the student has problem in this area. It is a combination of factors occurring together, over a period of time and to an extreme degree that should be the cause for action.

In the area of student hyperactivity, the teacher may consider implementing the suggestions provided in dealing with attention deficit disorder. The teacher can determine if those suggestions can make a difference. If the student begins to be less restless in the school the problem may take care of itself. If not, action beyond the classroom should be discussed with school administration and parents of the student.

The indicators mentioned previously describe students who have problems with attention because they are extremely hyperactive. Many students will show some of the indicators of hyperactivity behaviours to some degree at one time or another. The teacher should only consider the student to have a problem if the amount and persistence of the hyperactive behaviour is beyond the expected of a particular developmental age.

Frequently parents will say the student was hyperactive before beginning school. However, when the student was expected to sit still for extended period of time, beginning in the first grade, the problems become more obvious.

When determining the cause for hyperactivity, neurological and physical disorders of all types should be ruled out. The situation at home should also be reviewed, since students with problems outside school are not always able to leave them behind when they go to school.

Hyperactivity behaviour and learning disabilities have been linked to the ingestion of foods containing additives (ie. artificial food colourings, and flavours, antioxidants, preservatives, as well as excessive amounts of sugar).

While hyperactivity and attentional-impulsivity deficits often accompany school failure, it does not necessarily follow that the student will have specific learning disabilities. Thus, it is important to make separate and independent decisions about these two problems.

Suggested Intervention

The teacher should review the student's behaviour over a period of at least two weeks in a variety of situations. Then using the indicators discussed previously, check those items which apply to the student for that period.

The teacher should also consider the amount of physical activity needed by an active child and be sure this is available. Studies have shown that when hyperactive students begin the day with a lively exercise using a lot of physical activity, they are better prepared to sit quietly and work than when they are required to settle in immediately.

The hyperactive student may also need more frequent breaks from sedentary tasks than other students. Rather than wait until the student is so fidgety that he or she becomes an annoyance to all the children around, the teacher should provide planned activity breaks. Allow the student to do active jobs in the classroom, such as straightening out chairs, or cleaning the board, rather than filing or helping to grade papers.

Some hyperactivity may be due to distractions which the student cannot screen out easily. Providing the student a space with fewer distractions may also help alleviate the problem.

Techniques to address specific behaviour disorders:

Sometimes the teacher may need to employ special techniques to address specific behaviours even when the probable causes are removed. If the students have learned inappropriate behaviours, they may need some time to learn more appropriate classroom behaviour. The teacher must bear in mind that it is not enough to discourage a behaviour; it is important to teach a substitute, more appropriate behaviour.

Disrupting in class – Speaking out of turn:

The teacher should take the student aside and explain to him or her what the teacher sees as the problem. Describe specific situations in which the students call out when it was not their turn, or when it was inappropriate to do so, such as during a film.

The teacher should discuss why the students may be behaving that way and provide alternative behaviours. Alternative behaviours may include;

Raising hand in air when the student wants a turn.

The student should make a note to remind him or her what he/she wants to say or to give to the teacher to consider if he/she is not called.

Holding up a card. These cards may indicate agreement or disagreement or anything else that might be appropriate.

When discussion begins the teacher may ask everyone who wants a turn to raise their hand and then list their names on the board. Discuss other substitutes for calling out.

Disrupting in class- Leaving seat

If the student has a problem staying seated for an appropriate period of time, the teacher need to determine how long the student can stay seated without difficulty. This can serve as a baseline. The teacher should discuss goals with the student for gradually increasing the period of time he/she must stay seated, but plan for some acceptable behaviour if in fact, the student has great difficulty staying seated as long as other students.

If the student gets out of his/her seat and does not disrupt others, it will make it easier on the teacher. Again, the teacher can try some other alternatives. The teacher can determine if it helps to segregate the student, or allow him/her to do some work standing instead of sitting.

Also, the teacher can give the students interesting in-seat activities to keep them attending.

One of the observations about hyperactive children is that they have not mastered good strategies for learning. Their deficiency appears to involve an inability to mobilize the sustained effort and control required to meet the demands of doing tasks, even when they are dull and repetitive. They need to develop more efficient ways to approach tasks and studying. It is possible for teachers to help students in this regard. When introducing work to the student it should be:

Goal oriented
Purposeful
Organized
Logically programmed.

Specific tactics for solving problems should be taught. This might include tactics such as using concrete for counting and measuring, using markers under lines to stay in place while reading, blocks to mark off study time, etc.

LANGUAGE LEARNING PROBLEMS: RECEPTIVE AND EXPRESSIVE.

The following are indicators of language learning problems.

At or close to age/grade level in most areas except for the understanding and use of language.

At least a one year language delay is evident

Appears to ignore what others say

Short attention span for listening to others

Needs more explanation than others before understanding what is said.

Needs to see a picture or demonstration before understanding.

Responds in appropriately to what is said.

Often misses the point of what is said.

Very concrete; misses subtle nuances of speech

Difficulty in learning new words

Avoid games if listening to words is required

Avoids situations, if speaking is required.

Sources of Support

School administrators: The teacher should first notify the School Administrators when a problem is identified and further assistance is needed. Following advice of administration decisions may be made as to how the teacher should proceed.

Any of the following may be useful:
Subject area specialists.
Reading teacher
Speech-language pathologist
Learning disabilities specialist

Family members should be able to provide a history of the problem and the current treatment or outside services the student is receiving.

Medical personnel should be consulted to rule out any physical illness or sensory deficit.

Criteria for action

The teacher should observe whether the student has shown any of the language difficulties discussed earlier. A combination of these factors occurring together, over a period of time and to an extreme degree, should be cause for action. In the area of language problems, the teacher may implement the earlier suggestions and see if they can make a difference.

If the student begins to show progress in his or her ability to speak and communicate with the regular classroom procedures the problem not require minor intervention. If not, action beyond the classroom should be discussed with the school administration. This area becomes increasingly important as the student leaves the primary grades where there is greater expectation for understanding and using language out of context.

Possible reasons

By the time children are five to six years-of-age, they should have adequate comprehension of spoken/oral language. The level of comprehension depends on age and environmental experiences. If they do not understand, they will generally ask for clarification. They are able to hold conversations, listen to and obtain information, and give information to other people. There are developmental sequences which are natural: a child will understand and use the active voice before the passive voice. If this progression does not occur, intervention may be necessary.

Before considering language learning as a problem, the teacher should ensure that the student has had an audiological examination to rule out a hearing loss. Even a temporary loss, due to a middle ear infection, could interfere with the student's hearing and cause problems in comprehension, and create difficulty in learning language.

Occasionally, students with adequate hearing, have difficulty understanding spoken language. If a hearing problem is not found then other medical considerations such as some central nervous system disorder should be considered. The teacher may investigate as to whether there may be other family members with severe language problems to ascertain whether genetic factors are possibly involved. The teacher may also check to find out if there is lack of stimulation in the home or if the student has emotional problems.

A complete history of the student's linguistic development is very important to analyze the problem and to serve as a baseline for intervention

Consider the age of the student. Younger students are more likely to have difficulty with abstract language concepts, longer and more complex sentences and understand some words out of context. This does not constitute a language problem per se. The teacher can compensate for the age factor by the level of language he or she uses, by speaking more slowly and paraphrasing and, whenever possible, by giving the student additional clues to what is being said.

Given the optimal speech-language environment, if at least four of the indicators referred to earlier are observed, the student should be referred for a more intensive language evaluation. The student should benefit from intensive, individual speech-language therapy which closely coordinated with the teacher and the home.

The teacher should determine whether the problem lies with auditory memory (when the students cannot retain the sounds/words that they hear long enough to contemplate an entire thought, or with word comprehension (where the student hears and remember but do not understand the meaning of the words).

Auditory memory

If the student has difficulty repeating whole words, the teacher can use phonic approach with drills to repeat single sounds. The teacher must remember that the goal is not for the student to name letters, the sounds the letters represent in spoken words.

Next, the teacher should get the student start practising putting two sounds together and have the student repeat them. When the students are able to repeat two sounds, they could go on to three. These do not have to form a word.

After the student can easily repeat three sounds, the teacher can move on to short words and do a variety of exercises:

Repeating words

Pointing to/bringing object word is said.

March spoken word to written word.

The next step is short commands. The teacher may need to illustrate first.

Prepositions make good exercises. The teacher can ask the students to put a ball in, on, beside a box. Also, the teacher can take a doll and ask the students to wash various parts of the doll or do different actions. The teacher should make the commands short and slowly.

Word Comprehension

The teacher should give the student a lot of concrete experiences, constantly name things. Can make lots of picture books of categories of objects (e.g., food, clothing, animals, parts of the body).

The students can be taught how to describe. The students can be given words for size, shape, texture, colour, number, speed; these exercises should be made very concrete.

Other projects

While students are having difficulty using spoken language, the teacher should give them many other opportunities for success with other means of language and communication. Some students can learn to express themselves using simple gestures and signs, and once the concept of language is instilled, they are able to quickly pick up spoken language.

Students with a language learning problem may enjoy music and be alert to environmental sounds; the primary problem is comprehension and use of a linguistic code. If this is so, the teacher should provide many pleasurable listening experiences for the student.

Sources of Support

School administrators: The teacher should notify the school administration when a problem is identified and further assistance is needed. Following advice of administration decisions may be made as to how the teacher should proceed. Any of the following may be useful:

Subject area specialist

Reading teacher

Speech-language pathologist

Learning disabilities specialists.

Family members may be able to provide a history of the problem and the current treatment or outside services the student is receiving.

Medical personnel should be consulted to rule out any physical illness, and sensory deficits.

SEVERE COMMUNICATION PROBLEMS

The following are indicators of severe communication disorders.

No sign of distracting behaviour toward another person

Little or no expression of feelings or emotion on face or body

Subtle approaches when wants something.

Communicates simply; points, pushes adult towards object.

Moves adult to his/her biding.

Protects or avoids item or task without indicating why.

Asks for items or help without interest in person approached.

Respods to requests, but without interest.

Suggested course of action

The teacher should observe the student over a period of time to determine if the student has several of the behaviours indicated earlier. If the student's problems persist, he/she should be referred to a specialist with the prior consent, and informed parental permission.

Possible reasons

These indicators primarily describe younger children who experience delays or disorders in developing the ability to communicate appropriately with other people. If the problem persists pass grade one there is a possibility of a more severe problem requiring the help of a specialist in child behaviour disorders, such as a psychologist or psychiatrist.

Physical or sensory deficits or the possibility of mental handicap must be ruled out. It is important to determine whether the behaviours observed have been typical throughout the child's life, or if they represent a recent change in behaviour. Also, whether the child has been showing steady, if slow, improvement or has maintained the same status over time.

The indicators, mentioned previously, are arranged developmentally, following an order of progression from the student with the most severe communication problem to the student who is beginning to show minimal communication ability but without the signs mutuality required for true communication.

Because children rarely behave consistently in this area, the list should be used to develop a profile of the student. The techniques suggested under Learning disabilities, Attention deficit disorders, and Language learning problems are also relevant here.

Some of the additional considerations for the student with severe communication include:

Consistency in procedures used and the personnel employed. Often these students will need to develop trust and a feeling of comfort with an adult before they will perform in a cooperative manner. For this reason, standard testing will rarely reveal their true competence.

Attending to the slightest clues the student gives, in order to determine when and how they are communicating, and to immediately give a response in order to reinforce the communicative behaviour.

In addition to many concrete clues, the teacher should provide physical assistance to demonstrate what the students should do.

Also, the teacher can encourage simple turn taking activities rather than staying with commands to which the student must respond. Encourage and teach a wide variety of communicative responses.

EDUCATIONAL DEFICITS

Indicators of Educational Deficits

There are a variety of school related areas in which students may show delays or deficiencies. Some of these may include:

Social/Emotional – Functioning in self-development and interpersonal relationships

Gross and Fine motor – Ability to control large and small muscle movements.

Language Development - Ability to hear, comprehend, speak, and write.

Auditory and Visual Perception – Ability to encode and decode auditory and visual stimuli.

Self-help - Ability to perform personal management skill.

Academic/Cognitive – Functioning in reading and mathematics.

Criteria for suggested action

The teacher should review the indicators listed and determine if the student has discrepancies of a year or more in any of the areas listed. The teacher may implement some of the earlier suggestions and see if they can make a difference. If not, action beyond the classroom should be discussed with the school administration and parents.

Reasons for the learning deficits:

Social/Emotional

Problems with interpersonal relation are very complex. It is very important to get as much information as possible. When did it begin, under what circumstances, what changes have occurred over time, currently what seems to make the behaviour better or worse?.

Gross and Fine motor:

Any number of factors can cause motor problems. The problem can range from minor, such as slight weakness in a limb, to severe, such as in the case of cerebral palsy. Even a minor motor problem can cause a student distress. It is, therefore, suggested that the student be given a complete neurological and neuro-psychological examinations to rule out central nervous system disorder. Other testing may be required. Children with diabetics may have difficulty with tactual discrimination. Students with visual problems may have unusual gait or appear awkward.

Language Development

Problems in language development may occur because of a problem with hearing, cognition, environmental deprivation, emotional disorder, or brain dysfunction. There are also children who are slow in development but may gradually catch up. If a student comes to first grade with language skills significantly different from the norm of the class, he or she will definitely need individual attention.

Auditor and Visual Perception:

Problems with perception are often related to physical problem. It is, therefore, critical to rule out any type of damage to the peripheral or central nervous system that could be causing the difficulty.

Self-help Skills:

In the early grades some children may be slow in this area because they do not have good models at home or because they have been overprotected. However, with peers to follow they should soon catch up. If they do not, the teacher should look for signs of motor problems or difficulties in other areas which can give the teacher some further clues about the student's behaviour.

Academic/Cognitive Skills:

Problems in the academic/cognitive skills area may be due to learning or attention problems, mental handicap, sensory disorders, or social/emotional, physical and environmental factors. All of these should be explored before determining a student's correct placement in a school, class or curriculum, or the type of method that will be used in remediation. The teacher's teaching style and the student's learning style will be both important if the student is to make progress.

Student Educational Assessment Screening:

Psycho-educational assessments have been discussed extensively in Chapter One of this book. Teachers may refer to assessment procedures in that chapter.

Motor Problems;

Gross motor problems are indicated when the student is clumsy; has an uneven gait, poor balance, and/or awkedness.

Fine motor problems are evident when students have difficult time with drawing and writing, cutting, tying, buttoning, or anything that requires the use of the hands in a coordinated manner.

Tactile and kinesthetic perception may also be a problem. Some children who cannot feel differences between textures, have excessive need to touch, and show discomfort when been touched.

Students with motor disorders may have problems with body image. They may lack awareness of the relationship among parts of the body and have difficulty with orientation in space and moving from one place to the other.

Sometimes students have problems in school because motor problems cause them difficulty and draw the attention of other students who may tease them, thus causing additional emotional problems.

Depending on the type and extent of the problem, there are a variety of interventions. For the more severe problems physical therapy or sensory integration therapy may be prescribed on an individual basis. Other students can be helped by dance-movement therapy which can be done with the entire class or smaller groups. This should be at a level where the student with difficulty can have success.

Problems with writing and cutting can be helped by the teacher giving the student opportunities for practice using easier tasks. The student may also need more time to complete the task and this should be considered Some students may be more uncomfortable; they benefit from time spent in the classroom copying letters or pictures on a chalkboard or by practising staying within lines using a large crayon.

Language Development:

The reader should refer to the earlier discussion on this subject.

Auditory Perception

In a quite room the teacher may make sounds, the source of which the student cannot see, and ask the student to indicate when he/she heard the sound by using some action such as raising his/her hand, dropping a bead in a can, etc. In these exercises it is not important for the student to understand the meaning of the sound, just that the sound occurs. Initial sounds should be loud, distinct and may extend for a few seconds. Gradually the sound should become softer, shorter, and more difficult to hear.

Sound Discrimination

The teacher should use exercises where the student has to indicate whether two sounds are the same, or different from one another. The teacher must start grossly different sounds and move on to sounds that are similar. Exercises here deal with sounds other than speech sounds.

Sound Identification

The teacher may have variety of noise makers. The student is allowed to experiment making sounds with noise makers, who and make their sounds out of the student's sight. The student must indicate which sound was heard. He or she can either touch a matching noisemaker or point to a representation on a chart. The student should also be taught to recognize common environmental sounds, e.g., doorbell, telephone, alarms, etc.

Speech-sound Discrimination:

Beginning with grossly different sounds and moving on to ones that are quite similar the teacher should make two sounds and have the student indicate whether they are the same or different. The teacher may consider using the:"Wepman Auditory Discrimination Test" for this purpose.

Sound Recognition

When the student can discriminate between two speech sounds present them with a sound and ask him/her to indicate each time they hear it in a word.

Reproduce pitch, rhythm and melody – The teacher should start with readily available objects or noisemakers and move on to where the student imitates using his or her voice.

Sound Sequencing:

The teacher should allow students to practice in repeating sound sequences. Begin with short, simple sequences and move on to longer sentences.

Visual Perception:

As with auditory perception it is important to begin with simple tasks and move on to those which are more complex. The ideas listed below can be modified and expanded to capture the student interest. The teacher should ensure that the student do not stay with a task beyond the time it hsa been mastered, if the student seems to lose interest. The teacher should be prepared with a variety of tasks in this area to move the student along.

Match shapes, colours, and numbers:

The teacher should begin with three dimensional shapes so the student can not only visualize them but feel them as well. In the beginning when the teacher is matching shapes they should all be the same colour to avoid any confusion. When matching objects, they should all be the same shape. The student should be allowed as much time as necessary to help make these connections. Once the student has the concept of matching, the items may be more varied.

Trace outlines of forms and pictures:

The initial exercises on this level involve moving a pencil or crayon between two lines. The lines go from being far apart to very close. The next step is to follow the outline keeping the pencil as to the line as possible. Students should also practice filling in pictures staying between the lines.

Recognize likeness and differences:

Students shown two pictures that are similar except for one part. The students are to recognize what is different about the pictures.

Identify missing parts:

Shown common objects, students need to recognize what is missing, e.g., a face without a nose, a car without a steering wheel or a bicycle without a pedal. If the students have a problem with word recall or drawing, the teacher can have a set of possible correct visual responses from which the student can select a correct one.

Object Recognition:

In a picture that has several items, the teacher can ask the student to point out particular items. The teacher should then move from simple to more complex pictures.

Object Description:

The teacher should show the student an item. The student should be asked to look at the item carefully. The teacher should then put the item away and ask the student to describe the item.

Self-help:

Students need appropriate motor and cognitive skills if they are to succeed in self-help skills such as eating, dressing, and toileting. If these skills are not at age level, the teacher must begin a step-by-step process to teach the student the procedures involved. A useful technique here is 'backward chaining" In this process:

Analyze the steps involved – task analyze

Select the step that is closest to completing the task

Allow the student, as independently as possible to complete that step.

For example, in the process of zipping a zipper the steps involve placing the two sides of the clothing together, inserting the tab of the zipper into the receptacle and then pulling upwards. To teach this task the teacher does the first two steps and brings the zipper almost to the top, so all the student has to do is complete the pulling. The teacher works backwards, until finally the student is doing the action from the beginning.

CHAPTER VII

EDUCATION OF ETHNIC MINORITIES;
DEVELOPING COMMUNITY SUPPORT.

Over the years, visible minorities and other ethnic communities both in Canada and in the United States have been concerned about the impact of the education systems on their children in the schools.

The school systems have been accused of institutional racism.

Minority students, especially Blacks and First Nation students are disproportionally placed in Special Education classes on the assumption that students from such groups generally have cognitive deficits and may benefit from Special Education placements. There is no empirical evidence to support the assumption that Blacks and First Nation people are genetically inferior as compared to their White counterparts, and therefore, are cognitively inferior.

In fact, there is no racial group or groups that have monopoly over intelligence. Intelligence is normally distributed in a population. As such, there are children with very superior, superior, high average, average, low average, borderline, and educable mentally handicap in both visible minorities and White populations. If that is the case, why is it that visible minorities are disproportionately placed in Special Education programming?

Environmental circumstances along with institutional racism may account for the problems that confront visible minorities in the schools. Historically, in both Canada and the United States, institutional racism had existed, where in some cases, there had been separate and unequal education to the disadvantage of the visible, ethnic minorities and women.

It is believed that Black people in the United States and Canada have been at-risk for over two centuries, though in recent years it appears that Governments in both countries have been making efforts to redress the situation.

In the Province of Nova Scotia, for example, the Graham Royal Commission (1974) had recommended that the Minister of Education should direct all schools to take special pain to ensure that members of minority and disadvantaged groups be neither excluded; and that such groups be encouraged to explore, and acquire knowledge and understanding of their heritage, culture, traditions and problems and their contributions to Nova Scotia society.

It is believed that, in the past, Blacks and other visible minority schools were staffed with less qualified teachers, inadequate teaching materials and less other resources. Moreover, the environment in which some, and not all, Blacks and other visible minorities come from may be less stimulating. How then do we expect the child who comes from the highly impoverished environment to do well in school as their White counterparts? Experts believe that intelligence is an indication of our adaptation to our environment. This adaptation involves how our genetic endowment are moulded or influenced by our environmental circumstances.

From the foregoing, it would appear that some Blacks, First Nations and other ethnic minorities in the school systems may be skills deficits, due to lack of necessary and sufficient environmental stimulation and exposure and not cognitive deficits. For example, if a teacher or a psychologist, asks a student from a ghetto what is meant by the word "sad', most of these ghetto kids know what "sad" means. However, if the same student is asked to explain what the word, "melancholy" means, most probably that student does not know the meaning or have never heard of the word, "melancholy". What appears to be lacking here is skill deficit and not cognitive deficit.

There is also the argument that the materials used in social studies and history, in particular, are too much focused on White Anglo-Saxon Protestants, and not sufficient emphasis is placed on Black and First Nation history and cultures, Where references are made to the history and cultures of visible minorities, they are made from the White Anglo-Saxon point of view. Visible and ethnic minorities are generally viewed as hyphenated Canadians or American. Moreover, psycho-educational instruments and some educational materials are loaded with cultural biases to the detriment of visible and ethnic minorities.

For example, consider, the Comprehension subtest on the Weschler Intelligence Scale for Children. A question on that subtest asks the student as to what is the right thing to do, if a boy or a girl who is smaller than him/her starts to fight with him/her? The correct responses to that question is, 'Just walk away" or "I will not fight back" If the same question is asked a student who comes from the GaDangme tribe of Ghana, he/she will respond, saying, "I will hit him/her back" While the psychologist will mark the GaDangme student's answer wrong, the GaDangme student's answer is correct within the context of the culture he/she was born and raised. Intellectual assessment is based on the assumption that the examinee has had full culture.

The dictates of the GaDangme culture suggests that one should not allow anyone young or old to walk over a GaDngme and get away with it. Is such a GaDangme student overly aggressive? The answer is "no". Is he/she suffering from cognitive deficit? To suggest that the GaDangme student is suffering from cognitive deficit is utter non-sense. Yet, the psychologist may mark that student's response as incorrect, but may also consider that student as aggressive. The psychologist may end up recommending ridiculous interventions, which the student from the GaDangme background does not need.

Likewise, I am of the opinion, from many years of experience working as psycho-educational consultant in the schools, that though many of the teachers and professional consultants were good people, and meant well, in general, most do not understand the visible and ethnic minority students due to cultural or sub-cultural differences,

Here in Canada, there was a case in one of the Canadian provinces where the writer had lived and worked for years. In this particular instance, a young student from the West Indies had frequently referred to the late Muhammed Ali as "uncle"during class discussions. The child's reference to Ali as her"uncle" was perfectly normal as children are expected to show utmost respect for their elders whether they are blood related or not in West Indian societies.

The White Canadian teacher who did not understand the West Indian culture suspected that something was wrong with the child. So, she referred the young West Indian child to the school psychologist for personality assessment. A referral was sent to the child's mother to sign so that the psychologist could assess the child. The mother of the child reacted angrily to such a request when she was presented with a referral form to sign. She believed her child had no personality problems; that her child's reference to Muhammed Ali as her uncle was perfectly normal. When child's mother told the writer about the problem, the writer contacted the teacher and explained that aspect of the West Indian culture to the teacher. As a result, the referral to the psychologist was cancelled. The child had no emotional or personality issues. It was simply a matter of cultural differences.

The next was the case of a first Grade Black student who was wrongly diagnosed as "educable mentally handicapped" by a White psychologist with a doctoral degree. The child came from what was considered to be good and highly accomplished family. Though the child's family had divorced, relations between the child's parents were considered to be very good. Thus,, the child was considered to be well-adjusted and happy, though he was shy and not comfortable with strangers.

While in the first grade, the child began to experience academic difficulties. The child's teacher made a referral to the school's psychologist who tested the child and concluded that the child's overall intellectual functioning was in the educable mentally handicapped range.

The psychologist's report surprised both the child's parents and friends, who believed that, at least, the child's intellectual functioning should be in the average range. The child's father confronted the psychologist about his observations during the testing, and how the psychologist arrived at the inferences he made following testing. The psychologist revealed that the child was very shy and hardly responded to the test questions. This rendered the test results to be highly questionable. The child's father asked the school not to use the psychologist's recommendations or test results or else he would take legal actions against the psychologist, the school and the School Board.

The child's parents then hired another psychologist at a later date, who tested their child. There were twenty points significant differences between the tests conducted by the psychologist appointed by the school and the one hired by the child's parents in favour of the results of the psychologist hired by the child's parents. At the request and firm insistence of the child's parents, the school implemented the interventions suggested by the psychologist appointed by the child's parents.

The good news is that with additional help from his parents and tutoring that Black child successfully completed his grade twelve and earned a Grade twelve academic diploma. Since completing Grade twelve, he has also earned a diploma in business administration from a recognized Canadian academic institution. He had also passed courses from a highly recognized Canadian university.

The question arises as to what would have happened to that Black student as the school was going to place him in a special education class meant for the educable mentally handicapped, if his parents had not intervened.?

First Nation students, I believe, are perfectly capable of doing well in school, given stable, stimulating and nurturing environmental conditions. Some of them may be skills deficit, due to their environmental conditions, and not necessarily cognitive deficit.

Students from Asia and the Middle East may show English language deficits when they first arrive in Canada or the United States. Parents of Asian students tend to have stimulating environments for their students. Such students, for the most part, do not end up in Special Education programs; and if some do, such placements are only temporary. The schools and teachers seem to have more positive attitudes toward Asian students than Blacks or First Nation students. Moreover, teachers seem to have much better expectations of an Asian student than a Black or First Nation student. Positive teacher expectations are likely to motive a student to succeed and enhance the child's self-esteem.

Suggestions

Blacks and other visible minorities should become interested and participate more actively in the education of their children. They should seek to work more cooperatively with the schools and teacher; and be active participants in school-community relations.

Educational Psychologists should be more culture sensitive as they provide services in multicultural environments. Intellectual and other psychological testing are predicated on the assumption that the examinee has had full cultural exposure. Psychologists should be sensitive to the cultural issues; otherwise, their test results and inferences made from tests are useless. When placing a minority student following a psychologist's recommendation, other issues and facts about the child must be fully and thoroughly considered.

Other school's professional and support staff should also endeavour to be sensitive to the culture and the child's environmental circumstances.

REFERENCE

Achibald, JoAnne,ed. Canadian Journal of Native Education. Vancouver : UBC, Vol. 21, no.2, 1975

Barmann, Jean, et al. Indian Education. Vol.1, no1. The Legacy. Vancouver Press: UBC Press, 1986.

Bermudz, Ralow, Psychmetric View of Culture and Context: Research on Test Bias; National Research Council, 1982.

Black Learners Advisory Committee. The Blac Report on Education Redressing Inequity, Empowering Black Leaners, Vol.2. Halifax: The Blac, 1994.

D'Oyley, et al. African Canadians and Other Minority Children and Youth ar-risk Five Systems and Strategies to stimulate survival and visibility. Vancouver: Multiculturalism, March, 2002

Harrell, J.P. Physiological Responses to Racism and Discrimination. NCBI: PubMed Central, 2003

Intelligence Test of Cultural Homogeneity: Assessment of Intellectual Functioning BITH-100. Wikipedia.

Graham, John F. Report of Royal on Education and Public Service and Provincial-Municipal Relations. Part K. The Universities Halifax: Queen's Printer, 1974.

Graham, John R and Nuglien. Handbook of Psychological Assessment. Google Book: ISBN 1264512, 2003

Psychological of Ethnic Minority Populations – Americans. Washington, D.C: Black Psychologists, November, 2003

Reynold, Cecil Bias in Psychological Assessment. An important Review and Recommendation PSOF, 2016

Reynold, Cecil and Ramsay. Understanding in Psychological Assessment. Minority Objection to Test Bias. PSOF. 2003.

Stern, Begg. Alternative Approaches to Assessments. NAP.eds., 1995

West, T, V et al.Cultural Diversity and Ethnic Minority Psychology. York: Social Personality Psychology, 2016.

William, A. Assessing Children: Implications, Attitudes Using Affective Misattribution Procedure. Journal of Cognition and Personality Development. 17:505-525

Developing Community Support

The purpose of the Community Based Support System is to provide school level assistance to staff as part of the overall effort to maintain the student in the academic mainstream. It is apparent that many interventions may be outside the realm of the school and require cooperative approach with other agencies. The school must be an integral part of a larger cooperative system.

In other to achieve this, each school building might have a Special School Advisory Committee consisting of community persons who have a variety of resources to support the student and the family. This committee might include: teachers and other staff, the local clergy, public health personnel, the probation officer, or members of any of the community support agencies that are available.

This is a building level group which would meet as necessary to discuss students' needs, and try to plan in-school interventions. This intervention could range from provision of material things such as lunch money to consultation with an advisor or counsellor. Where necessary, outside resources may be used, but only when all efforts within the school have been exhausted.

The primary objective of this effort, are maintenance of the student in the local school and to provide help to the classroom teacher so the teacher can feel an integral part of the support service and have the help as well as the responsibility for the student who is at risk of school failure.

A community support system should always be in place, ready to be called upon as needed. Such a system is the responsibility of the school, since the teacher does not usually have the time or the authority to create a system, nor is usually the prerogative of a teacher to intercede directly with an outside agency for a student.

The teacher should be alert to potential problems and try to anticipate the interventions that might help prevent the need for removal of the student from the classroom or school if the problem becomes unmanageable. To this end, community support should be enlisted when needed and for a wide diversity of students. As often as possible, the service should come into the school to strengthen the service or the school's resources.

Keeping in mind that no entity can serve range of needs that might require attention, suggested solutions are:

Investigate what health, mental health, and resources units of various types, already exist in your area;

Develop a resource directory including each agency. This should be done by a committee consisting of teachers, parents, and school wide staff such as the counsellor, social worker, and psychologist. If the school works closely with some agencies for services, those agencies should also be involved. in the planning.

One person or a small committee should be designated, in the school, to be responsible for the updating of the Directory, and as the contact person with the community agencies should a teacher needs assistance.

Any agency that can provide an educational, therapeutic, health, recreational or social services to a student at risk should be contacted with an explanation given that the teacher is interested in preparing a list of services that could be available if required for a student in that school.

Schools that have already use this approach and found it useful, might be willing to help others in their Community Support Directory.

School Referral Procedure for the Teacher

Contact the person in the school who is the designated contact with community agencies and discuss the community resources that could be beneficial for the student and his/her family.

The designated contact person should contact the agency to obtain specific details regarding the availability and appropriateness of the service in this particular case.

The family should be contacted, the problems and the possibility of community resource discussed with them, and then assistance provided to help them obtain the service. Also, follow-up assistance if needed.

The family will then have to sign a form allowing the school to release information to the agency about the student. This information should include the teacher analysis of behaviour symptoms, the Student Referral and other forms specific to the student's difficulty.

In turn, an arrangement needs to be made for the school to be able to get feedback from the community agencies regarding their findings and suggestions for possible interventions to take place in the classroom.

ABOUT THE AUTHOR

Dr Joseph Nii Abekar Mensah was born and raised in Accra, Ghana. He received his basic education at Saint Mary's Parish School and Accra Bishop's Boys' School, Accra, Ghana. Dr.Mensah then attended Odorgonno Secondary School in Accra, Ghana

Upon completion of his secondary school education, Dr. Mensah was sent by his late father Nii Larbi Mensah II to London, England, where he studied Applied Biology with specialization in Pharmacology at Barking Regional College of Technology, Dagenham, Essex, England. He later worked as a Research Technologist at London Hospital Medical College, University College Hospital Medical School and Union International, London, England.

Dr. Mensah later immigrated to Nova Scotia, Canada, where he was a Research Technologist at the Department of Pharmacology, Dalhousie University. Dr. Mensah later earned undergraduate and graduate degrees in Education and Psychology at Saint Mary's, Dalhousie and Mount Saint Vincent Universities; and at Columbia Pacific University.

He had served as a Part-time lecturer in education at Dalhousie University; as an Adjunct Faculty at the University of Santa Barbara and Columbia Pacific University; and has worked extensively as Psycho- educational Consultant.

Dr. Mensah is the author of a number of books, including, STRESS MANGEMENT AND YOUR HEALTH and TRADITIONS AND CUSTOMS OF GADANGMES OF GHANA: DESCENDANTS OF AUTHENTIC BIBLICAL HEBREW ISRAELITES.

Printed in the United States
By Bookmasters